EXCLUSION

EXCLUSION

Strategies for Improving Diversity in
Recruitment, Retention and Promotion

NATALIE HOLDER-WINFIELD

Cover design by Elmarie Jara/ABA Publishing.

Printed in the United States of America.

18 17 16 15 14   5 4 3 2 1

Library of Congress Cataloging-in-Publication Data

Holder-Winfield, Natalie, author.
  Exclusion : strategies for improving diversity in recruitment, retention, and promotion / by Natalie Holder-Winfield.
      pages cm
  Includes bibliographical references and index.
  ISBN 978-1-61438-865-4 (alk. paper)
  1. Diversity in the workplace--United States. 2. Discrimination in employ-ment--Law and legislation--United States. 3. Multiculturalism--Untied Staes. 4. Personnel management--United States. I. Title.
  KF3464.H63 2014
  658.3008'0973--dc23
                          2014003410

Discounts are available for books ordered in bulk. Special consideration is given to state bars, CLE programs, and other bar-related organizations. Inquire at Book Publishing, ABA Publishing, American Bar Association, 321 N. Clark Street, Chicago, Illinois 60654-7598.

www.ShopABA.org

Contents

PROLOGUE

Most good interviews about workplace politics start by someone saying, "Let me close my office door." When I reached out to Susan de las Cuevas* to have a beyond-the-brochure conversation about her experiences as a woman of color in a Wall Street financial firm, I expected to hear egregious stories about men behaving badly. Financial services, which is still a male-dominated industry, had a reputation in the 1980s and 1990s of being like a college fraternity.

> "The only real conflict you will ever have in your life won't be with others but with yourself."
> —Shannon L. Alder
>
> "Love your Enemies, for they tell you your Faults."
> —Benjamin Franklin, *Poor Richard's Almanack*

After embarrassing exposés about client outings to strip clubs, multimillion-dollar class action lawsuits for gender discrimination in promotions, and being the textbook definition of a hostile work environment, during the early twenty-first century, most firms got serious about internal compliance and governance. Today, it is a challenge to visit a major financial firm's website and not see a statement of diversity and programs for small women-owned business. Although the industry has made a marked shift toward eroding the old boys' club, in 2010, I was still able to find an article—"Sex Harassment at Work Gets Weirder, Scarier"—filled with horrifying accounts of violent, degrading, and embarrassing acts against women that led me to believe that Susan would add to the qualitative data I was collecting around diversity, inclusion, and retention.[1] However, her

---

*Denotes that the person's name was changed to protect his or her identity.

more noisome stories came from an unexpected place: a not-for-profit in the Northeast.

Susan is one of those enterprising and resourceful types of professionals. In college, as a communications major who had never taken a business class, she was able to convince a bank to turn an unpaid internship into a summer job paying her fifteen dollars per hour. When she graduated from college, she was a permanent fixture on Wall Street, working in private equity and finance, and on trading desks. The glimmer of the financial world gave her travel, social, and networking opportunities that many of her neighborhood friends would never experience. The first time that she "took a car home" after a long summer day in the office, the people on her block stopped and stared as she stepped out of the black Lincoln Town Car. Susan had made it. That is why her mother, a first-generation American with fading ties to Puerto Rico, did not understand how her daughter could one day walk into her apartment and announce that she was leaving a job with a hefty salary to work for a nonprofit. Susan explained to her mother that she was offered a job by a national organization that does exactly what she loves: advancing the careers of college-age students. However, she had no idea that her ethnicity would be such a focal point for derision and compartmentalization in this nonprofit.

She felt like an outsider for the first time in her career when she joined this nonprofit, especially when one coworker in particular reminded her as such. Let's call this coworker The Nemesis. During a staff breakfast, The Nemesis wanted to make everyone laugh and said to Susan, "We are not serving rice and beans for breakfast. Are you still hungry?" On another occasion, at a national staff conference, The Nemesis asked Susan to translate a brochure into Spanish. When Susan explained that she was not bilingual, The Nemesis joked in the presence of colleagues that she was a LINO (Latina in Name Only). (The Nemesis's assumption that Susan spoke Spanish is ironic because she would often tease Susan about being sheltered, assuming that Susan had never traveled outside of the United States.)

The stereotype of a Latina from the Bronx followed Susan all the way to the leadership ranks of this organization. Here is where she converted their unaware misconceptions of her skills and background into a career advancing strategy. Her supervisors were always polite and cordial with her and never intentionally tried to make her feel uncomfortable. However, her supervisors believed that her Spanish-origin last name made her an expert on Latin Americans. She used their assumptions to her advantage. By feeding into their image that she could be their Latina spokeswoman, she engaged in a bit of chicanery and used this as an opportunity to pivot her role into a high-level national position. During our interview, she quietly whispered that all of her promotional titles included the word "Latino" in them, hypothetically "Director of Latino Affairs" or "Senior Leader of Latino Outreach." She admitted that she never encountered the level of blatant use of her demographic identity in the banking industry. She explained, "I have been treated as a minority in this environment and I was made to feel othered because I didn't share the predominant ancestry of the majority—African Americans."

Susan's experience illustrates a well-known but rarely acknowledged shift in the twenty-first century workplace: Most discriminatory acts are wrapped in an invisible package called micro-inequities. The blatant has been replaced by a chimera of subtle but insufferable behaviors that leaves one wondering, "Is it me or did that really happen?" Further obfuscating the issue of unfairness is the complexity that various demographic groups can be the dominant majority in an organization such that no demographic group has a monopoly on bias and the ability to exclude.

The incongruity of The Nemesis's actions sounded schizophrenic the more I learned about her. She is an African American woman who has committed her life and education to creating academic and professional opportunities for Latinos. Actually, the nonprofit was dedicated to the professional success of Latino college students. Undoubtedly, The Nemesis was truly committed to the Latino students that she helped over the years. In fact, many of her former students publicly expressed their gratitude for her writing recommendation letters, helping them to prepare for interviews, answering their weekend telephone calls when they were anxious about their performance in an interview, and making the vote-of-confidence telephone call to an admissions officer that got them into their first-choice college. Yet, while working with Susan, it was clear that she was aware of the stereotypes (i.e., cognitive representations of culturally held beliefs about out-group members) about Latinos, and they oozed out in intimate office settings and at large conferences. The Nemesis' condescension begs the question: how could someone so committed to working *for* Latinos be so offensive when working *with* a Latina?

The answer to this question lies in a truth that many of us will only admit when proven with neuroscience and social psychology—none of us are immune from bias. We all possess prejudices (i.e., the negative affective responses toward out-group members), and if left unexamined and challenged, we increase our chances of engaging in the subtle discrimination that forms micro-inequities.

INTRODUCTION: WHAT EXACTLY ARE MICRO-INEQUITIES?

We often build our public image, reputation, and self-perception to conform to societal norms. Given the legal, political, and social pressures that squash public displays of bias, today you risk becoming a social pariah for discriminatory conduct. As a result, blatant discrimination is becoming harder to find in our professional work spaces. There are strong social desirability pressures not to discriminate on the basis of race and many other protected classes. In addition to numerous fair employment statutes, states like Connecticut and California have taken an extra precaution against discrimination by enacting laws that require managers to receive mandatory sexual harassment prevention training, which often includes training about prohibited discrimination against other protected classes such as race, national origin, disability, and religion.

> "People's perceptions of the world—and of themselves—are often shaded toward maintaining a positive view of themselves."
> —Freud cited by Michael I. Norton, Joseph A. Vandello, John M. Darley
> *Casuistry and Social Category Bias*

The civil penalties for discrimination are both monetary and reputational. Celebrities, athletes, and high-profile CEOs are popular examples of the social outcast one can become for engaging in discriminatory behavior. Isaiah Washington played the cocky and brilliant Dr. Preston Burke on ABC's *Grey's Anatomy* until he got into a verbal tussle with a cast member, calling him a derogatory word used to describe gay men. Shortly afterward, he was written out of the show and most of his subsequent work in Hollywood has gone straight to DVD. In 2006, Mel Gibson found himself on the talk show circuit not to plug a new movie but instead to apologize for anti-Semitic remarks. And who could ever forget Fuzzy Zoeller's stereotypical jokes about then twenty-one-year-old Tiger Woods serving fried chicken and collard greens at the Masters Champions Dinner. While these men may have once been household names, after their controversial outbursts, their names are more likely to be used as a learning moment at the kitchen table. Endorsement deals, social acceptance, and a desire to think that we have evolved are just some of the motivations for not appearing prejudiced.

Yet no amount of legislation can prevent the human nature tendency to create us (in-group) versus them (out-group) dichotomies and actively separate ourselves from people who seem different. As human beings, we have a natural inclination to look for and align ourselves with the familiar. The next time that you walk into a party, take a moment to observe how people splinter into groups. Most likely you will find that there is some thread of similarity that binds each group. The concepts of in-groups and out-groups are not new and are so commonly understood that they are rarely debated. However, it is the bias and favoritism that stems from them that stumps most leaders who seek to create inclusive and performance-driven organizations.

Bias is an interpretive judgment of how we see others, and it is not necessarily based on anything objective or empirical. Bias motivates our preferences. We move into the intergroup bias territory when we systematically value our own membership group (the in-group) or its members more favorably than the out-group.[2] Being an outsider stems from intergroup bias that can range from stereotyping and prejudice to discrimination. Although bias is anathema to organizational mission statements, it is also human nature. Subjective uncertainty reduction theory, which explores how we try to eliminate the unfamiliar from our interactions, explains that we are more inclined to choose friends, spouses, and even employees that we identify with.[3] With similarity, there are fewer perceived differences and the increased likelihood of comfort and fewer perceived conflicts. To feel comfortable, most of us automatically seek to eliminate the unknown in our social and interpersonal interactions.

In-group bias travels along a continuum that starts with favoritism and a preference for others in your group. Have you ever heard someone express that he or she did not trust someone of another race solely because that person was of another race? Or express hesitation about bringing someone from a different demographic group into his or her inner circle? Our inclination to trust members of our in-group is grounded in an initial form of discrimination based solely on in-group favoritism.[4] At the other end of the in-group bias spectrum are more aggressive actions and hostility, which entails an active component of aggression and out-group derogation. When someone from an out-group violates in-group norms, that person may elicit disgust and avoidance. An out-group seen as benefitting unjustly may elicit resentment and actions aimed at reducing benefits from the in-group. That is why diversity-related programs are sometimes met with resistance by a dominant majority in the workplace that views these programs as preferential treatment for nondominant out-groups—women, people of color, people with disabilities, etc. And, an out-group seen as threatening may elicit fear and hostile actions. When A Better Chance (ABC), the nonprofit that seeks to place students of color in boarding and day schools, was expanding into Ridgefield, Connecticut, there was a huge uproar. The initial cohort would consist of ten to fifteen Black and Latino girls. While the Ridgefield residents never said that they did not want those "Black kids" in their neighborhood, they vociferously objected to the ABC program because they did not want that *New York City element* with all of the problems of an urban environment, e.g., drugs, entering their bucolic community. Needless to say, including Black and Latino boys in the inaugural cohort was a nonstarter.

Along with dominant in-group status comes privilege. "Privilege is usually unconscious and invisible to the individual graced with it, and privilege is exercised unknowingly and assumed to be a natural right."[5] The identities that gave us entry into the in-group become what is considered as "normal." For example, the pantyhose color "nude" is a natural and neutral color for some while brown would be closer to nude for others. When we are in the in-group, the balance tilts in our favor for small benefits (e.g., grooming styles) and larger benefits (e.g., the ability to avoid out-group members and to be a part of the dominant group). The privilege of being in an in-group is that we possess a characteristic that elevates our status and we don't even think about. For example, while women may feel marginalized when their gender puts them in the out-group, heterosexual women enjoy in-group status because their sexual orientation belongs to the dominant group. The same woman who might feel denied of opportunities because of her gender probably gives little thought to how she has the privilege of being in heterosexual romantic relationships that are considered "normal." That in-group characteristic is what makes it possible to exclude and deny status, opportunities, and something of value to out-group members. The Nemesis probably did not realize the privileges she held by being in the dominant in-group of this nonprofit. The organizational norm made it safe to point out Susan's Hispanic ethnicity and poke fun at it.

Why do we create in-group and out-group distinctions if we know that they can unfairly exclude others?

The overwhelming body of research from the field of social cognition makes it irrefutable that people "possess attitudes and stereotypes over which they have little or no conscious, intentional control."[6] Pioneering researchers in Harvard's Project Implicit have developed tools to show that we may not speak our minds because we do not always know our minds.[7] Their Implicit Association Test (IAT) measures attitudes and beliefs that people may be unwilling or unable to report. Scientists have found that we have access to only 5 percent of our conscious minds, while the majority of our decision-making takes place in our unconscious implicit minds.[8] Psychological social studies have revealed that, sometimes, the disconnect between our actions and our private subconscious thoughts is rooted in our not being consciously aware of our beliefs—socially acceptable or not. This is why in the early twenty-first century, in academia and psychological research, the IAT gained traction for studying and identifying our uncontrolled reactions to demographic stimuli.

The IAT is a timed sorting task that measures the strength of associations and attitudes of our automatic responses to a range of stimuli: mental health, race, gender, sexual orientation, disability, Arab-Muslims, presidents, and a host of other demographic areas. This computerized test measures cognitive reflexes by timing the test participants' response to positive and negative attributes associated with a chosen characteristic. The diagram below is an example of the IAT categories when the test taker chose to test his implicit bias toward race.

Category	Items
Good	Joy, Love, Peace, Wonderful, Pleasure, Glorious, Laughter, Happy
Bad	Agony, Terrible, Horrible, Nasty, Evil, Awful, Failure, Hurt
African American	faces of African American people
European American	faces of European American people

The goal of the test is to go as fast as you can to categorize a word or a picture when it flashes across the screen. For instance, if the computer key "e" is assigned to the words that fall into the "good" category and the "i" key is assigned to words that fall into the "bad" category, when the word "joy" flashes across the computer screen, you would click the "e" key as fast as you could. If instead you hit the "i" key, your response would be incorrect. When African American is paired with the good qualities, you should strike the "e" key; however, if instead you hit the "i" key, that would be recorded as an error.

The illustration on the following page by Jonathan Ziegert and Paul Hanges's study, *Employment Discrimination: The Role of Implicit Attitudes, Motivation, and a Climate for Racial Bias,* is a good example of how this test works.

In the first test (diagram of Trial 1), the target categorizations (White and Black) were introduced, and then in the second (diagram of Trial 2), the attributes (pleasant and unpleasant) were introduced. Throughout the experiment, test participants will see various pairings of the racial groups and the attributes. In one trial, the negative attribute is paired with Blacks and the positive attribute is paired with Whites. Words will flash across the screen (e.g., sickness, death, paradise) and the test participant will indicate by pressing the keyboard whether he or she associates these words with the Black-negative or White-positive pairing. In the

RESEARCH REPORTS

Trial 1: Initial Target Categorization

Sample Stimuli

WHITE		BLACK
✔	HEATHER	
✔	ANDREW	
	ALONZO	✔
✔	EMILY	
	LATONYA	✔
	TYREE	✔
✔	HARRY	
	TAWANDA	✔

Trial 2: Initial Attribute Categorization

Sample Stimuli

pleasant		unpleasant
	sickness	✔
✔	freedom	
	death	✔
✔	miracle	
✔	happy	
✔	paradise	
	prison	✔
	disaster	✔

Trial 3: Initial Combined Categorization

Sample Stimuli

WHITE or pleasant		BLACK or unpleasant
	ALONZO	✔
✔	paradise	
	disaster	✔
✔	HEATHER	
✔	miracle	
✔	LATONYA	
✔	ANDREW	
	sickness	✔

Trial 4: Reversed Target Categorization

Sample Stimuli

WHITE		BLACK
✔	LATONYA	
	ANDREW	✔
	HARRY	
✔	ALONZO	
✔	TYREE	
	EMILY	✔
✔	HEATHER	
✔	TAWANDA	

Trial 5: Reversed Combined Categorization

Sample Stimuli

WHITE or pleasant		BLACK or unpleasant
✔	sickness	✔
✔	miracle	
✔	ALONZO	
	LATONYA	
	disaster	✔
	ANDREW	✔
✔	paradise	
	HEATHER	✔

next part of the test, the pairings are reversed, such that Black and positive are paired and White and negative are paired. Again, words will flash across the screen (e.g., prison, happy, freedom) and the test participant will indicate whether these words are associated with the Black-positive or White-negative pairing. Researchers have determined that implicit bias against Blacks exists if the test participant takes longer and makes more errors when Black-pleasant are paired than when Black-unpleasant are paired. (And, implicit bias against Whites exists if there are more errors or there is a longer response time when White-unpleasant is paired than when White-pleasant are paired.)

Research has even gone beyond surfacing our implicit biases and delved into defining the distinctions between the various types of implicit biases—implicit stereotyping vs. implicit evaluative bias—in an effort to better understand predictive responses, outcomes, and opportunities to create policies.[9] Implicit stereotyping occurs when we unconsciously ascribe our own historical understandings of a person and make judgments about him or her based on our prior experiences with the group we associate that person with. For example, we decide to not invite the single mother in our department for drinks on a Friday night because we assume that she has to take care of her children and will not attend. We have made a judgment about her without giving her the opportunity to prove us otherwise. Implicit prejudice is the evaluative bias that motivates us not to include the single mother in office conversations, to interrupt her while she is talking in a meeting, or to treat her coldly. Implicit prejudices are subtle prejudicial slights, such as avoiding eye contact, hesitation in speech, and overall less friendly behavior. By analyzing our neural circuits, scientists have found that implicit prejudice is learned more quickly and unlearned more slowly than implicit stereotypes.[10]

Societal stereotypes about race get ingrained in our memories as young as three years old, and they usually come from our social influences: parents, peers, and the media.[11] Justin Levinson's Duke Law Review article *Forgotten Racial Equality: Implicit Bias, Decisionmaking, and Misremembering* found that:

> As people grow older, their stereotypes become implicit and remain mostly unchanged even as they develop nonprejudiced explicit views.[12] Stereotypes about ethnic groups appear as a part of the social heritage of society . . . [And] [n]o person can grow up in a society without having learned the stereotypes assigned to the major ethnic groups.[13] Most people probably do not realize the extent to which they discriminate, however, because they are acting on unconscious biases—whether cognitive (race and other group-based stereotypes), motivational (the desire to maintain and promote the interests of

their own group), sociocultural (internalized societal values, beliefs, and traditional), or a combination thereof.[14]

For example, researchers have found that although the American ideal of meritocracy dictates that race and gender should not be factors in decision making and our judgments, "race and gender are automatically attended to and encoded almost instantly, suggesting that their influence on decision making may be hard to avoid."[15] Social psychology professors Darley, Norton, and Vandello conducted an experiment where a man and a woman were candidates for a construction job. When the genders of the candidates were not revealed, 76 percent of the participants chose the candidate with more education. However, in the second round of the experiment when the genders of the candidates were revealed and the female candidate had more education, only 22 percent of the participants ranked education as the most important criterion.[16] The specious reasoning that the research participants used to justify their questionable behavior of ranking education important until it inured to the benefit of the women is called *casuistry*.

Casuistry helps to explain The Nemesis's moral hypocrisy—the dissonance of engaging in self-interested behavior at a cost to others.[17] While she saw the importance of supporting Latinos in their professional lives, she still saw Latinos as an out-group. At times, she was unable to restrain her unconscious deep-seated biases and made off-color jokes about Susan. Sometimes our prejudicial decisions are masked and rationalized in other ways to avoid the appearance of seeming anything less than egalitarian.

One theory as to why we possess implicit biases stems from a desire to maintain social order, creating "a direct link between a culture of racial subordination and implicit racial bias."[18] Social Dominance Theory (SDO) "proposes that society contains ideologies that either promote or attenuate intergroup hierarchies. Individuals with a high SDO have a strong desire to promote intergroup hierarchies and for their in-groups to dominate their out-groups."[19] According to this theory, majority groups will have a high SDO. For example, in terms of global power, men have a higher SDO than women. Whites will have a higher SDO than Blacks. Heterosexuals will have a higher SDO than homosexuals. In Susan's situation, because African Americans were the dominant group in her office, they had a higher SDO than Latinos. The Nemesis wanted to maintain the dominance of African Americans and she did so through condescending humor that was intended to keep Susan in her place.

Some have argued that to focus on unconscious bias is to lose sight of the real issues that will help society achieve its justice goals. In a 2009 *Emory Law Review* article, Ralph Richard Banks and Richard Thompson Ford argued that "Despite its ostensible political benefits, the unconscious bias discourse is as likely to subvert as to further the cause of racial justice . . . The unconscious bias discourse reinforces a misguided preoccupation with mental state, and perpetuates an obsession with anti-discrimination law, rather than policy reform, as a means of realizing racial justice."[20] The argument continues that we know our racist attitudes and beliefs, but we hide them from researchers. The contention with unconscious bias is that it allows us to supplant the covert racial bias that still exists with a more palatable notion of unconscious bias, which "levels neither accusation nor blame." Calling bias implicit, unconscious, and anything that occurs voluntarily is deemed as "misdescribing" the issues of bias that we still battle today. Others believe that "old-fashioned racists" have morphed into modern-day racists who are motivated by social norms to hide their prejudice.[21]

Paula Deen, host of the Food Network's *Paula's Home Cooking* and America's favorite southerner is a good example of the debate Banks and Ford present. Her show was cancelled after court deposition documents revealed that she used the N-word and was planning a plantation-style wedding for her brother, complete with Black servants.[22] Although Deen apologized a number of times via YouTube after her clandestine inter-office conversations became headline news, many debated whether she suppressed her racist biases all these years or was an unknowing victim of the thoughts and ideologies of a different time. Many gave her a pass under the unconscious bias rationale: how could Paula be held responsible for something that she didn't even know she was doing? In fact, a much ridiculed group of African Americans created a website called "Black People for Paula" and were scheduled to host a rally in Times Square in support of Deen. (Regardless of this fringe group's efforts, as of the date this book went to print, Deen was still a disgraced former cooking-show host.)

While I agree that some of us may be more conscious of our biases and hide them in mixed company, there are people who really are not aware that they harbor biases, prejudices, and stereotypes. After Susan left the nonprofit, she had an opportunity to tell The Nemesis about how she made her feel. Susan's Nemesis never realized that many of her "jokes" were offensive stereotypes of Latinos and apologized profusely.

Whether acts of exclusion occur consciously or unconsciously is inconsequential. The aim of this book is to make clear the connections between bias—in any form—and the impact it has on the success of individuals and organizations. In other words, the origin of the bias is less important than the fact of its existence. What complicates the narrative and makes this book so critical is that the nature of bias is changing. There are no giant billboards or clear signposts. We can no longer predict or assume who will demonstrate bias or where or when we will encounter it. And yet, the social, political, and economic consequences are as relevant as ever. My goal is not to let anyone off the hook or keep anyone on the hook. Throughout this book, I will create the trifecta connection between inclusion, engagement, and retention for organizations that will help erase any reason or excuse for not being able to advance their diversity initiatives. I will provide case studies for identifying when out-groups exist such that those who feel marginalized can develop the strategies to say, "I do not feel included." Instead of wondering whether exclusion occurs consciously or unconsciously, I want to get at the objective heart of the retention dilemma: the ten most common micro-inequities.

"Micro-inequities" is a term coined by MIT professor Mary Rowe, who explained, "Discriminatory micro-inequities are tiny, damaging characteristics of an environment, as these characteristics affect a person not indigenous to that environment. They are distinguished by the fact that for all practical purposes one cannot do anything about them; one cannot take them to court or file a grievance."[23] They are the gestures, tone of voice, or other behaviors that subtly tell you whether you are valued and accepted or deficient and an outsider. Micro-inequities have the ability to diminish one's self-esteem and lead one to question his or her capabilities.

Similar to beach erosion, you may not see micro-inequities every day, but you see their impact over time. Based on hundreds of hours of interviews with junior to seasoned lawyers, architects, doctors, professors, university administrators, television personalities, and a host of other professionals, I found that there are ten reoccurring micro-inequities:

1. informal mentoring
2. misperceptions about their performance
3. the quality of their work assignments
4. insensitivity
5. dual identity
6. bullying
7. the ability to recover from mistakes
8. first generation hurdles
9. isolation
10. assumptions, slights, and other annoyances

There are probably millions of other subtle actions that communicate inclusion and exclusion. However, I found that these ten micro-inequities occurred with a frequency that created identifiable categories. When you can detect an issue, you increase the likelihood of being able to correct and prevent it.

While any person can be on the receiving end of micro-inequities, my research comports with that of other researchers who have found that the likelihood of encountering micro-inequities increases the further you are from the dominant in-group.[24] That is, women, people of color, people with non-American accents, people with disabilities, the LGBT (lesbian, gay, bisexual, and transgender) community, and non-Christians are more likely to encounter micro-inequities. Throughout the book, you will read examples of how these micro-inequities manifest themselves in organizations.

Further, the amount of money that organizations spend on diversity-related matters persuades me to give senior leaders the benefit of the doubt that they really do want to see improvements in the diversity of their workforces. Each year, organizations collectively spend millions of dollars on recruiting and retention efforts—some with a heavy emphasis on diversity. Since 2000, there has been an explosion in organizations hiring chief diversity officers and creating roles to support diversity efforts. The average salary for a diversity executive is above $100,000, and often this person reports directly to the CEO or president of the organization.[25] Plus, most organizations understand that there is a business case to diversity and inclusion. As you can see from the chart below, there is a huge price to pay when organizations do not have a workforce that under-

Figure 1: The rise in buying power by diverse groups

	1990 Buying power	2014 Buying power (projected)	Increase between 1990 & 2014
African American	$318 billion	$1.1 trillion	246%
Hispanic	$212 billion	$1.3 trillion	513%
Asian American	$117 billion	$696.5 billion	495%
Native American	$19.7 billion	$82.7 billion	320%
White	$3.8 billion	$13.1 trillion	245%
(LGBT) Lesbian, Gay, Bisexual, Transgender	Not avail.	$835 billion	

*Source: The Multicultural Economy 2009, Selig Center for Economic Growth
*Source: The Buying Power of Gay Men and Lesbians 2008, Witeck Combs Communications

"In the new economy, the best people are the most likely to leave. Why? Because they can. And they are likely to leave long before they've paid their dues or even paid a return on your recruiting and training investment."
—Bruce Tulgen, *Winning the Talent Wars* (W. W. Norton & Company, 2001)

stands, connects with, and can appeal to America's changing demographic: Even if Ford and Banks are correct in their assertions about unconscious bias, there is a conscious war for customers and talent that reflect America's changing demographic.

RETENTION AND MICRO-INEQUITIES

It is well known that most employers want a workforce where their employees feel connected to their work and the organizational mission. According to a 2012 Society of Human Resources Management survey, 600 managers expressed that employee engagement was their second highest priority.[26] Yet, in 2012, Gallup's Employee Engagement Index polled 1.4 million employees and found that nationwide only 30 percent of employees were engaged and nearly one in five workers was actively disengaged.[27] Why is employee engagement so important to organizational success? Researchers have found that employee engagement affects nine performance outcomes, including higher productivity, higher profitability, and higher customer metrics.[28] When you connect employee engagement to Mazlow's theory of self-actualization, the engagement-performance outcomes make sense.

Abraham Mazlow was a psychologist whose research found that humans are motivated to fulfill a level of needs before they can move on to more advanced needs. At the base of this hierarchy of needs are our basic human needs to eat and sleep, and our other survival needs. The next level in this hierarchy is our security needs such as steady employment, shelter, and health care. However, it is this next level of needs where an organizational environment has great impact. Our social needs are fulfilled when we feel as though we belong. When we have friendships and other relationship attachments in the workplace, this creates the difference between the person who is looking at his or her watch all day and cannot wait to go home versus the person who feels accepted. Acceptance encourages our involvement in the social community of our workplaces, e.g., committees and contests. The next level of needs, our esteem needs, when fulfilled gives us a sense of accomplishment. It is when our team recognizes our contributions and gives us a greater sense of self-worth. And lastly, once all the other needs are met, we may get to the level of self-actualization. This is the highest level in the hierarchy of needs. This is where we are concerned with our potential growth and are obsessed with fulfilling our potential. Because we have been equipped with confidence about our work, we care much more about the outcomes and will obsess over creating solutions to the organization's biggest problems. This is the level where our creativity is unleashed and we are capable of devising new products and services. Steve Jobs, Oprah Winfrey, and Mark Zuckerberg are good examples of individuals who are/were self-actualized in their industries and felt confident enough to initiate bold and courageous products and services. They are also entrepreneurs who started and ran their own enterprises. In existing and established businesses, it is possible to foster innovation as well.

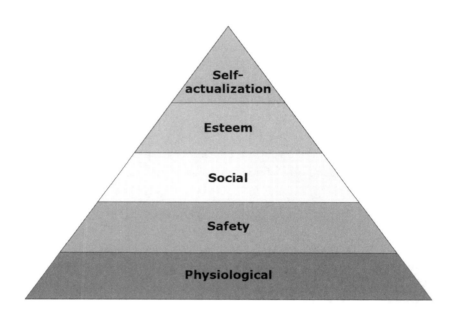

However, if employees feel like outsiders because they are battling the micro-inequities of managing bullies, insensitivity, or isolation, their social and esteem needs are probably not being met, which means that they will probably never reach the level of self-actualization.

While we are well equipped to notice when others harbor biases, we often deny that we too have biases and create out-groups.[30] The asymmetry between how we view ourselves and how we conduct ourselves is the glaring contradiction

> "The best antidote to unconscious bias is self-reflection."
> —Drew Westen, psychologist and neuroscientist, Emory University[29]

that leads us to engage in micro-inequities.

Aside from intentional conduct and those who have no interest in increasing diversity, most people fail to create inclusive cultures because they do not realize when they are members of a dominant in-group and do not know how to bridge alliances with out-groups. Often, they do not know how to relate to out-groups.

Another challenge to creating the inclusive environment that would yield a more engaged and self-actualized workforce is that in-groups do not know the actual experiences of those who have felt marginalized. To get people to truly understand and respect each other, there must be a common experience to which we can all relate. What is the common denominator experience that most of us can relate to regardless of race, gender, ethnicity, disability, or any immutable characteristic?

At some point most of us have felt like the outsider and felt as though we did not fit in with a group. Have you ever been in a situation where you were the only person with (or without) a particular characteristic? Have you felt like the "only one" while riding on a subway or bus, or while driving through a different part of town? Did you move to a different neighborhood so that you would be among people who shared your culture? Were you the only person dressed inappropriately at an event? While these examples may seem trivial, have you avoided feeling like an outsider when you could? Have you called a friend before an event to ask what he or she was going to wear? One of the first times that I realized the extent to which people will avoid being an outsider was when I invited a client—an executive recruiter who wanted to meet more attorneys—to a complimentary reception for women of color who were in-house counsel for Fortune 500 companies. She declined. Although these women were within her target market, she thought that she would not feel comfortable at the reception because she feared that she would be the only Jewish woman in the room.

Many of us have felt as though we were a part of a group because of our race, gender, ethnicity, color, disability, socio-economic status, style of dress, or political affiliation. When you found yourself in a situation where you noticed that you were the only person with a characteristic, you were in the nondominant out-group. How did you feel? Uncomfortable?

Self-conscious? Usually we feel as though we don't belong when we are a person in the minority, and that feeling is only multiplied when someone screams it to us in their action and behavior. Once it is confirmed that we are not wanted by a group, we lose interest and stop investing our time, energy, and passions.

I developed the *Top Ten Micro-inequities* model to compile and describe the common experiences, thoughts, feelings, stories, and issues people encounter that make them feel like excluded outsiders.

Exclusion is based on conversations and interviews with professionals from a wide range of fields. I spoke with lawyers (naturally), advertising sales executives, authors and editors, scientists, marketers, doctors, nurses, military personnel, financial executives, accountants, and so on to gather their experiences of being a person in the minority. It is a resource that managers can use to figure out how to get their high-potential employees to feel less like outsiders and reach the self-actualization level.

This book is divided into ten chapters, each devoted to one of the Top Ten Inequities that outsiders encounter. The people who shared their experiences and feelings did more than provide case studies, so I prefer to see them as more than just research subjects. They are people. Some may feel that the interviewees' stories are negative whining. However, it is just this type of assessment that inhibits outsiders from sharing their experiences, and these are the experiences that would truly advance organizational diversity, inclusion, and performance. Further, whether or not they are whining and being negative, these are the reasons behind organizational attrition, and these are the barriers that stand in the way of your employees feeling self-actualized and engaged. Their testimonials bring to life the common syndromes of workplace adversity and how sometimes the feelings of exclusion damage a person's self-esteem and sense of self-worth—the emotions underlying their employment dilemmas and complicated career decisions.

The testimonials are invaluable for their honesty. The people I interviewed shared raw feelings and thoughts that your employees would never share with you (at least while sober or if they want to keep their jobs). The professionals I interviewed wanted to forge healthier relationships with their majority colleagues and managers. Some of the people I interviewed found ways to survive in environments that are far from welcoming and developed survival mechanisms that are worth sharing. Some interviewees found alternative paths for success and are working for organizations that fulfill their personal and professional interests. Through their testimonials, you will get a sense of their frustrations with working in environments where they had to fight to get recognition for their hard work. You will get a sense of their supervisors, who even with an organization-wide diversity and inclusion initiative, just didn't get it.

It may seem at times that my book is for lawyers. However, this book is for anyone who has ever felt alone and marginalized or for anyone who seeks to become an ally in the quest for inclusive workplace cultures. I conducted hundreds of hours of interviews with employees from a variety of industries: health care, engineering, media, financial services, nonprofit. As a lawyer, it was easy to use the legal profession to create examples and learning opportunities. I used the legal profession, which struggles to become more inclusive and diverse, as a glaring example of the pitfalls and barriers to creating more diverse environments. (According to an American Bar Association study, almost 100 percent of women of color leave their law firms within six years of practice.[31])

VALIDATION

Employees can learn so much from the interviewees' testimonials. For starters, you will realize that you are not the only person to experience dual identity, the absence of informal mentoring, and the other Top Ten Inequities. Many of the people I interviewed did not get mad when they encountered a barrier; they got smart. The stories shared by the interviewees should be used by the employee-reader to similarly take charge of his or her career.

This book is also intended to include White men in the dialogue about diversity and inclusion. Often, the literature and programming around this topic does not create a space where White men can relate. I recall attending a "Diversity Reception" where the host corporation's general counsel's compelling argument to create such a space was saying, "White men, give up some of your power." I would rather create a paradigm where White men can empathize, rather than sympathize, with historically underrepresented professionals because they too have encountered micro-inequities and exclusion based on some dimension of their identity.

SOMETIMES WE DON'T KNOW WHAT WE DON'T KNOW

By naming the micro-inequities, there is an opportunity to learn about them and not be caught off guard by them. Most colleges and universities focus on job placement, providing industry seminars and business seminars about the career search, but rarely can they provide programming that prepares their students for the realities of the workplace. Most career services offices do a great job of organizing diversity panels and cocktail parties that inspire students. However, it is almost impossible to host frank discussions about the disappointments, challenges, and adversity that professionals in the minority encounter. How often are there discussions about cliques and favorites in the workplace? Sometimes your demographic identity, not your performance, determines whether you are in the in-group. This is not an easy topic to discuss without anonymity. Regardless of the mistreatment a person has endured, we know better than to name names under any circumstances. We do not tattle on those who made our lives miserable—and sometimes literally created our demise.

This book exposes professionals and students to some of the best-kept company secrets about marginalization. As Malcolm Gladwell wrote in *Blink: The Power of Thinking without Thinking*, when people have a chance to understand and anticipate what is happening, their reactions are better informed.[32] In the book, Gladwell describes a training exercise where bodyguards were assigned to a program referred to as "stress inoculation."[33] Basically, the bodyguards were repeatedly put through a test where they were shot with plastic bullets and attacked by ferocious dogs. The test was conducted over and over again. The first time the bodyguards were faced with an emergency, they could not think straight and panicked—"mind-blindness." However, by the second and third times the exercise was conducted, the bodyguards' reactions improved. The repetitive nature of the exercise combined with real-world exigencies took the surprise out of the encounters and the bodyguards were able to respond much better. The preparation gave the bodyguards the skill to slow down and to keep processing information. As Gladwell wrote, "This is the gift of training and expertise—the ability to extract an enormous amount of meaningful information from the thinnest slice of experience."[34] With advanced warning of the *Top Ten Micro-inequities* that people of color, women, people with disabilities, LGBT professionals, immigrants, and people from any other underrepresented backgrounds in the workplace encounter, you won't be as shocked and mind-blind if and when you encounter a similar situation.

Finally, I gathered a few expert opinions to weigh in on the dialogue. Chai Felblum, Commissioner of the Equal Employment Opportunity Commission, shares her insights on the *therapy* that some managers need to be effective. Governor Dannel Malloy of Connecticut talked to me about managing bullies. In chapter 1, you will read about a study conducted by researchers from the Wharton School of Business, Columbia School of Business, and New York University who found that implicit biases show up in professors' decisions to answer e-mail requests from prospective PhD candidates of different races and genders. In that chapter you will read about what some institutions have done and the progressive actions that were taken once these biases were determined. And, former *Essence* magazine editor and image activist Michaela Angela Davis provides an intriguing paradigm for shifting the responsibility for being conscious about differences.

While the book offers advice for removing the Top Ten Inequities, remember that each organization is unique and has its own culture. Consider what will and will not work in your organization before you apply any of the principles in this book to your own situation.

CHAPTER TAKEAWAYS

- The Top Ten Inequities model compiles and describes the most common experiences, thoughts, feelings, stories, and issues people encounter that make them feel like excluded outsiders.
- Aside from intentional conduct and those who have no interest in increasing diversity, most people fail to create inclusive cultures because they do not realize when they are members of a dominant in-group and do not know how to bridge alliances with out-groups. Often, they do not know how to relate to out-groups.

- No amount of legislation can prevent the human nature tendency to create us (in-group) versus them (out-group) dichotomies and actively separate ourselves from people who seem different.
- Casuistry helps to explain our moral hypocrisy—the dissonance of engaging in self-interested behavior at a cost to others.
- Societal stereotypes about race get ingrained in our memories as young as three years old, and they usually come from our social influences: parents, peers, and the media.
- The overwhelming body of research from the field of social cognition makes it irrefutable that people "possess attitudes and stereotypes over which they have little or no conscious, intentional control."[35]

CHAPTER 1
THE POWER OF INFORMAL MENTORING

After what seemed like a series of marathon interviews, you were finally offered your dream job. The night before your first day of work, your emotions may have ranged from anxious to excited to nervous. Then finally, the big day came where you walked into the building as the new employee. Do you remember how foreign everything and everyone felt to you on your first day of work? Although you may have known how to research the latest news or create spreadsheets of yearly projections, you may have felt directionless until someone gave you your password and taught you how to access the company's computer network. You were also stuck until someone showed you where to sit, gave you your company identification, told you where to find office supplies, or showed you how to record your time. By the end of your first week, you probably started to feel more relaxed, and with each passing day everything seemed less new (and less daunting) to you. Imagine if every day you felt as untethered to the workplace as you did on your first day of work. This is how it can feel when you do not have an informal mentor (or a truly engaged formal mentor).

In addition to having someone help you master the technical administrative chores, you needed a mentor to introduce you to the organization's corporate culture. You needed someone to tell you about the boss's finicky likes and dislikes. You needed someone to help you understand the right time to propose a new idea and how to package it such that the department welcomed it with open arms. We all need someone to invest themselves in our success. Whether your field is law, business, or medicine, you need a mentor.

Karen Brown,* a former Assistant US Attorney, has been the recipient of the investments an employer will make in an employee's success.

1

Only in her early thirties, she has felt the difference between a boss who obsessed over her career and a boss who couldn't care less.

> I think that there are three kinds of people: people who are interested in your success, there are people who are indifferent, and there are some who are out to sabotage. Luckily, I have only met with the first two. I think that for my first two or three years with the government I worked for someone who was not only interested, but obsessed with my success such that I got great work. And when I did well, I got praise for it and my supervisors and colleagues knew about it. I came to have a reputation as doing good work. Judges knew me and colleagues knew me to be someone with a good head on her shoulders.

In her last year and a half working for the Department of Justice, Kara worked for someone who was more or less indifferent. While he did not seem to mean any harm, Kara noticed the different dynamic.

> I think there's another level to it when you're a minority because when I sit across a desk from someone who's not Black or a woman, there's an assumption that we don't have an understanding of one another because he or she doesn't look like me. And then we may talk, and find out that we have much in common and that we can work together and even hang out and have a great time. But from the moment I sit down, I don't look anything like you; you probably perceive my experience to be very unlike yours. I just think that you really need a cheerleader in your profession. It's too hard, it's too competitive not to.

Very few organizations would dispute the importance of mentoring for its ability to facilitate the vital information exchange between senior- and junior-level employees. (Although they do disagree as to whether involuntary mentor-mentee pairings truly work.) Numerous articles have been written about formal mentoring programs and the radical results they have produced in the business world. Within the last twenty years, companies like AT&T's Consumer Sales Division, Boeing, and Deloitte & Touche have created corporate universities that include creating the structure for and giving substance to the mentor-mentee relationship. According to a *Fortune* magazine article, corporations experience half the turnover rate and a 55 percent increase in performance by sending their managers to corporate universities.

However, are all employees given access to the same opportunities for informal mentoring? Regardless of formal mentoring programs, people still gravitate toward people they naturally like and create bonds with them. In 2009, researchers at the Stanford School of Business authored a paper titled "Common Ground and Cultural Prominence: How Conversation Reinforces Culture," which found that most people would prefer to have conversations that are familiar to them and, as a result, search for familiarity. The researchers determined that the most prominent people in your organization are not always the ones producing the highest-quality work; they might just be better at selling themselves.[36] This is the essence of what leads us to lean toward informally mentoring within our in-groups. By sharing in-group status (whether it is along lines of race, gender, school affiliation, etc.) we share a point of similarity that creates familiarity.

Many of us have an innate desire to work with people who are familiar to us in some aspect of our demographic identity. We choose to go to lunch with certain individuals as opposed to others because we may share common experiences with them and find it easy to talk politics, our children, or our love for ethnic foods. We invite coworkers to our summer barbecues because we may have gone to the same schools and share an alma mater. We invite the woman down the hall to the theater because she has a great sense of style. We invite the new guy to the Knicks game because we enjoy the same sports. Ultimately, we play and work with people we like.

Katherine Milkman, PhD, is a Wharton Operations and Information Management professor whose leading research on our instincts and judgments sheds light on how and why we decide to help others. When I came across some of Professor Milkman's work, the words "fun" and "quirky" came to mind. Her Wharton website biography describes her research as, "rel[ying] heavily on 'big data' to document various ways in which individuals systematically deviate from making optimal choices. Her work has paid particular attention to the question of what factors produce self-control failures (e.g., undersaving for retirement, exercising too little, eating too much junk food) and how to reduce the incidence of such failures." Now that sounds like a way to spend your day.

When I reached out to her via e-mail on a Saturday morning for an interview, she responded within minutes. When we spoke a few days later, I understood why she was so motivated to pursue her brand of research. When Professor Milkman looked around her PhD program, she noticed that all of a sudden the minorities and women whom she spent so much time with in college were not there anymore. Once she got to the doctoral level, and particularly when she was looking up at faculty who were mentoring doctoral students, she was startled by the lack of diversity and wanted to understand why there was a dearth of women and students of color. That's what sparked her research in discrimination and management. In 2012, she embarked on a project to research how and when professors respond to e-mailed requests for a meeting from unknown prospective doctoral students, which she calls a *pathway* moment in one's career that could negatively affect diversity.

> Diversity officers tend to focus on what we call *gateways*. So diversity officers will focus on asking "how can we have a more fair and objective process for evaluating candidates at the point of application, say for a job or PhD program?" That is where a lot of their time is spent. It is at these gateway moments where there is an official process for making a decision and they can focus on improving that process. What we're trying to highlight in our research is actually that there are many *pathways* leading up to gateways where we receive informal encouragement; advice that is valuable about how to structure our application; and how to write an excellent research paper or dissertation that might lead to getting a job. We receive informal mentoring. Those pathway interactions are not going to be monitored typically by diversity officers. Those are processes that we engage in on an ad hoc basis: decisions we make as faculty without consulting a rulebook or, frankly, using any objective criteria. We simply use our instincts.

Professor Milkman collaborated with Modupe Akinola of Columbia University and Dolly Chugh of New York University to design an experiment in which they sent e-mails to 6,500 professors at 258 US universities representing 89 different disciplines. The names of the fictional prospective students were randomly varied to indicate whether the sender was a man or a woman, or if he or she was White, Black, Hispanic, Indian, or Chinese. In some of the requests, the student asked if he or she could come in for a meeting that same day; others asked to meet in a week.

When the researchers, posing as students, tried to schedule a meeting with a professor within one week, White males were 26 percent more likely to successfully schedule a meeting and 16 percent more likely to receive a response than all of the other demographic groups. While some

Student Race and Gender	E-mails Ignored		Meetings Denied	
	%	% Increase Relative to Caucasian Males	%	% Increase Relative to Caucasian Males
Caucasian Male	26.5%	N/A	52.4%	N/A
Caucasian Female	29.8%	12.5%	52.9%	1.1%
Black Male	32.5%	22.6%	61.3%	17.0%
Black Female	34.4%	29.8%	60.0%	14.6%
Hispanic Male	36.9%	39.2%	58.2%	11.1%
Hispanic Female	27.1%	2.3%	55.7%	6.3%
Indian Male	41.8%	57.7%	68.2%	30.2%
Indian Female	37.7%	42.3%	67.9%	29.7%
Chinese Male	36.7%	38.3%	66.8%	27.6%
Chinese Female	46.9%	77.0%	62.9%	20.2%

Copyright Katherine Milkman, Modupe Akinola, and Dolly Chugh 2012

professors were outraged that they were duped into participating in this study, the results force us to examine the unconscious biases that drive our instincts to respond to requests to mentor some and not others.

During our conversation about her findings, Professor Milkman shared, "Even in my own presentations of this research at academic conferences, one of the most frequent responses that I get from faculty in the audience is, 'Wow, I never thought about the fact that when I simply rely on my judgment to decide who to spend time with and who to help when I get these requests, that is an opportunity for bias to creep in. This is going to change the way that I respond to e-mails and meeting requests in general and think about mentoring and these ad hoc opportunities to be helpful to students.'"

So how do we increase our chances of getting mentored? "Looking Up and Looking Out: Career Mobility Effects of Demographic Similarity Among Professionals" is another study conducted by Professor Milkman, in collaboration with her mentor, Harvard Business School Professor Kathleen L. McGinn, that offers useful strategies. While many will say that your mentor does not have to look like you, Professor Milkman's research of large law firms indicates that there is value to having a mentor who shares your demographic traits.

> I looked at law firms and work groups and the effects of work group composition, particularly demographic composition at the top level. So, examining whether who the partners are in your group factors into your likelihood of staying in the firm if you are a junior lawyer. One of the things we looked at if you're a junior woman, for instance, and you're in a work group with very few senior women is the question: does that help or hinder your chances of being promoted and staying in the firm? And, what we found was that having senior sponsors who are the same gender was really important for female attorneys and their likelihood of staying and also in terms of promotion prospects. So that suggests that there still are benefits to having a mentor who shares your demographics, and we are not the first to show this. In fact we're simply replicating well-known phenomena just in a more modern setting.

Ultimately though, she encourages people to have multiple mentors who can understand your demographic-specific problems as well as a mentor who is demographically different from you but may have a stronger network of connections. Then you get the best of both worlds.

> It would be wonderful if we lived in a world where we didn't need sponsors who shared our demographic traits especially because minorities and women tend to have fewer network connections in

general, and so if you're looking for a mentor who is well-connected, you're probably best off with a White man. However, there are benefits that accrue from having someone as a mentor who looks like you and can understand your problems, which may be unique. For instance, imagine you are a woman having a child and there is a different expectation at home about what you'll be doing and what portion of the work you'll be taking on, and you have a male mentor and you want to talk about that. You may not get the same benefits as if you'd had a woman mentor who had the same experience, just to give an example. I think until we overcome that, which may never happen, there will be benefits to having mentors who look like you and who can understand and relate to the problems that you're struggling with.

Benita Serles,* despite her cheery smile and good sense of humor, has always felt like the odd person out in her office because of her race. Although she feels as though she is welcoming to her colleagues—who were all White—she believes that they have rejected her over and over again because they could not identify with her. "I've never worked in a situation where I was not in the minority. Sometimes it's hesitation or not being included in any social events. I know that it's not exactly related to work, but in the ultimate analysis it is. It's just not ever being invited out to the Thursday or Friday evening after-work party. There were times when someone made a mistake and asked, 'Are you going to the bar after work?' I felt out of the loop."

As Benita noted, during these informal meetings—those "spur of the moment" outings—informal mentoring is taking place. When someone is tapped for an unspoken membership in someone's "in" club, he or she automatically becomes privy to vital information that is exchanged within that circle. The more elite the circle is, the more powerful the information exchanged will be. New projects and opportunities are discussed and assigned. What happens when some people are invited to impromptu lunches with supervisors and others are not? What happens when some people are continuously not invited to have drinks after work? Can a formal mentoring program overcome the advantages of informal networking?

Shawna James* emphatically says no. She dabbled as an attorney for a large law firm before striking out on her own and starting a lucrative law firm practice. Her petite stature and Shirley Temple-style locks often fool her adversaries into thinking that she is an easy opponent. However, she is one of the Washington, DC, area's top-notch corporate transaction attorneys. Although it has been over five years since Shawna worked for a big law firm, her matter-of-fact description of her summer associate experience and the lack of mentoring are crystal-clear memories that she will not soon forget.

> I can recall not being mentored when I was working for a firm in the Midwest. I went to school in Atlanta and I was an outsider because most of the people were from the area. I also noticed that there was a tight-knit connection between some of the attorneys and the summer associates who were not racial minorities. Obviously there were general opportunities that were given to all of the summer associates. We were all invited to the College World Series, we were all invited to basic firm-wide events, but in terms of making personal connections or connections that would allow the attorneys and the partners an opportunity to get to know us on a personal basis—opportunities that would have given them additional information about making hiring decisions after we completed our summer associate positions—that did not happen.

How does one overcome an office clique that is created by upper management? It's difficult enough when coworkers band together to create an in-group and exclude others, but it is even worse when it is the supervisor or owner of the company who decides to carve out social opportunities for some employees and not others.

Lisa Charles* realized in her first real job after graduating from Duke University and Columbia Law School that the workplace was not created equally, especially if the boss cannot identify with you. Lisa worked for an international law firm and had every intention of becoming a law firm partner. She kept her head in the books while the law firm partners were tapping her colleagues on the shoulders for higher caliber opportunities.

Slowly, Lisa noticed that all work and no play was something that the partners determined as her destiny. By giving a little nudge to serendipity, Lisa was able to find a job with a bar association where she is actively involved in the workplace and social functions. When Lisa looks back at her experiences at the firm, she recognizes how a mentor would have brought her on a partnership track.

When I was at my firm I definitely felt excluded. It even goes back to when I was a summer associate. I was the only woman of color in a class of thirty-five to forty summer associates. That was very challenging and it was not as though I was overtly excluded, but there were very different social activities that I was not used to. Most of the social activities revolved around drinking. That was how folks socialized and got to know each other. There weren't social activities that I was more comfortable with.

Partners definitely made relationships with White male summer associates. Their relationships were based on so many things that were not about work. It was based on going out drinking together during lunch. It was based on going to each other's homes. Partners were inviting White male associates to their homes, and I didn't even know about it until well afterward. People were taking associates out to lunch, informally. I was not a part of any of that. As summer associates, we would go out together and then occasionally the senior associates would take groups out so that they would get their lunches paid for.

These relationships that were made between the partners and the associates were at the partner's initiative. It wasn't the summer associate going to the partner, which you sometimes hear you have to do. It was the partner inviting certain people. It happened among the White male members of my class, and it was about people feeling some sort of connection in terms of "This person reminds me of myself when I was a first year" or "This person reminds me of how I was when I was younger." A White male is never going to say to a Black woman, "Oh, you remind me of how I was when I was younger." There was no one in that leadership role that could say that about any person of color. That's part of the identity, right? And the familiarity? Race is part of that. Ethnicity is part of that. Being male or female is part of that. That's part of the identification. Unfortunately, there were no Black women partners or Black partners, period. There was one Asian partner who came later. Those informal mentorships started within the first six months of being at the firm. I was not a part of that.

I didn't really know these informal relationships were going on until well into my second year. I didn't really notice it and I didn't realize how important it was. That's one of the things that if I could go back and do it again I would do differently—the politics of working at a firm. I didn't really appreciate how important the politics were. I didn't realize it was going on around me until it was too late. By the time I realized that people were forming these friendships and relationships that are much more beyond the business context, it was too late. It wasn't until I saw that there were one or two people who were identified in my class as "really great people to work with" who I knew were not necessarily the smartest people. I worked with them, and I knew that their work was OK. They made mistakes when I was working with them. I began to see how certain people were given work because the people who were being promoted had the right people behind them. The people who are still at my former firm are people who were identified in their first year as people who were going to make it.

Brock Douglas,* an executive for an entertainment company, encountered a similar situation of exclusion when he worked in the automotive industry. To his surprise, and dismay, not even his MBA from the Wharton School of Business kept him from being excluded from his supervisor's inner circle. "What's interesting is that things have gotten more subtle. Here's an example from a previous employer where there was this whole notion of not being in the circle. In a sense the circle was created by my boss where she handpicked people. When I joined her group, I came along as someone she had not handpicked. The organization was restructured and she had to deal with me. She had to accept me into the fold."

Some of the resistance from his supervisor was that the people in her organization were men and women she was comfortable with. They would spend time together on the weekends, they would go out to dinner together, and it felt like they were sons and daughters of the female boss who ran the group. Brock's out-group status was multi-layered. First, he was an outsider because the boss did not hire him. Second, he had the barrier of being the new kid on the block.

The lack of informal mentoring micro-inequity manifested itself most notably in his supervisor's resistance to travel.

> What expense-related events I traveled to and whether I needed to go to certain events was questioned. I felt like there was a level of scrutiny that was applied to me that was not applied to her close-knit group. Because my boss controlled the purse strings, she made decisions about what, and where I attended events. I didn't see this type of questioning of my colleagues who weren't even going to events that were as germane to the business. It just felt like they had been going to these events for years and there was a wink and nod of approval. They were either going to events with her or they were going with people that she knew who were also in the circle, so it made it easier for her to say their events were legitimate but mine were not.

In the end, he felt like he needed to be chaperoned in a way that others were not.

Interestingly, when I suggest to companies that I include mentoring advice in the employment education programs I have been hired to present, they confidently assure that "All of our employees have access to the same opportunities." These organizations believe that since they have mentoring programs, all of their employees have a mentor in the organization.

Yet, as Kathleen McDonald* reveals, mentoring is sometimes based on what you look like and not necessarily who you are. Kathleen is a caramel-colored Caribbean woman who wears her hair naturally curly. Motivated to become an attorney because of the intellectual challenge it presented, she started her career path at Harvard Law School. She spent the earlier years of her career working for an international law firm in New York City where her office was ensconced in Wall Street's financial center and bordered by the Statue of Liberty and the East River. Although Kathleen's firm had a formal mentoring program, she noticed how many of the White partners informally socialized with her White male and female colleagues.

> Whenever it came to social events, going to the theater, a sporting event like a golf event or so on, there was always a set group of individuals who were always sent invitations. But someone like myself was never on the invite because they just felt like the events were something I would not be interested in even though no one ever consulted me on the issue. I would hear about it after the fact, like, "So and so went golfing with this particular partner." The in-crowd was White and willing. They were Caucasian for the most part and they said yes to everything. It didn't matter what it was, they were very good at schmoozing.

Even though Kathleen was applauded for her work, she was left out of those impromptu outings after work or on the weekends. These impromptu meetings were where her colleagues were creating closer relationships with the firm's leadership and were positioning themselves to work on the high-exposure projects. Kathleen's interactions with the partners were mostly limited to office meetings and a quick hello while passing in the hallways. After five years of working for this firm and feeling as though none of the partners had even an inkling of interest in her career, she left the firm to open her own law firm.

Everyone I interviewed about mentoring expressed the importance of having a champion in the workplace. Incidentally, all of the people I interviewed worked for companies that had formal mentoring programs, yet there were noticeable differences in the way they were mentored versus their colleagues who resembled senior management.

Now we are left with the questions, How does an organization overcome the disparities caused by informal mentoring? How does an organization control natural bonds between senior- and junior-level employees and ensure that all employees are similarly mentored? As the senior-level person, are you guilty of mentoring only people who remind you of yourself or your children?

As the testimonials indicate, subtle gestures to mentor some people and not others are blatantly obvious. When people feel overlooked, they stop investing in the organization. Each time an employee leaves, it potentially costs the organization thousands in training and recruiting. Can your organization afford to lose valuable talent because a manager could not figure out how to schedule at least one outing a month—whether it's dinner or a casual office meeting—with all of the employees in a group or division with whom he or she closely works?

Informal mentoring is simple enough that any busy executive can effectively master it. The gathering does not have to be anything extravagant. It could be as simple as a fifteen-minute, one-Monday-a-month meeting in your office to discuss recent goings-on and make sure that your employees do not have any questions about work. Sometimes, but not all of the time, a telephone call will do. Or, it could be a matter of inviting the employee to your home to have dinner with your family. Of course, the more genuine and frequent the gatherings, the better, but employees will appreciate any effort toward mentoring that does not appear to be forced.

During a training session, I was inspired when a manager was humble enough to admit that he had left some employees (the problem employees) out of his informal mentoring network and that he needed to "reset the clock" with them. If you are a manager who has a reputation for inviting employees to events outside of the workplace, you should try to include different employees. As a manager, if you are concerned that you will not have anything to talk about to your employee, try talking about yourself. Junior- and mid-level employees read books about captains of industry and are eager to learn how to advance within an organization. Surely, your employees would be interested to learn how you navigated your way through the organization. Similar to the anecdotal advice you offer when speaking on a program panel, you could impart this information to your employees.

Former Senior White House Advisor and New York University Provost Melody Barnes understands that as a senior-level woman in government, she is always mentoring others.

> Quite frankly, the thing that consistently motivates me is this idea of "lifting as we climb" and the fact that so many people took time out of their day to help me and continue to take time out of their day to help me. One of the things I realized after I left the White House was the number of young women who pay attention to what you do, everything from how you handle a meeting to what you wear and what you chose not to wear. One day I was joking with my deputy and told her that since my days at the law firm I have three rules about socializing professionally: one-piece bathing suit, two drinks, conservative dancing. Later, all of these younger mid-level women in the White House were coming up to me and saying, "I heard your rules and I am following those rules." I had no idea that I was sharing some great piece of information.

As a frequent commentator on MSNBC, it is easy to imagine how often people reach out to Melody for advice and guidance. Yet, she has found a way to avoid feeling inundated.

> I had to develop a filter so I could manage it, support people in a meaningful way, and not become overwhelmed by what my husband calls my side business of mentoring that has nothing to do with the business that pays the bills. I am focused mainly on those I've worked with and that's the core group of young people that I will spend a great deal of time with. With others, I may have a conversation, they'll ask me a series of questions, and I will try and provide feedback. In some cases, we may have a follow-up meeting every quarter or something along those lines, but that's the way that I've learned to try to manage it from a time management standpoint.

ATTRACTING MENTORS

While being in the out-group can create a challenge to being mentored, there are a number of strategies that successful professionals have used to endear themselves to champions who will obsess about their careers.

Sometimes we attract our informal mentors through our passion and enthusiasm. You have probably seen the big navy blue with yellow trim Achievement First banner if you have driven through Hartford, New Haven, or New York City. Those schools owe a lot of their success to its founder and CEO Dacia Toll, and she owes a lot of her success to her informal mentors.

> Very early on when we were starting the original school, Amistad, I went to New York and I met with Dave Levin, who was at the time running what is now the biggest charter network in the country. And I also went to Newark and I met this guy Norman Atkins, who was running North Star. Dave and Norman were ahead of me by a couple of years. We became very good friends. They were mentors, friends, and doing the work, and they have been extremely important. I learned a tremendous amount from them. I've had a tremendous number of board members who have made an investment in developing me and the organization that I run. With Dave and Norman we were doing the same work. It was the sense of we want to help our kids. It was never about the specific work that you're doing; it was about a mission. Dave, Norman, and I even started a teacher university together.

Marcella Nunez-Smith, MD, is a professor at the Yale School of Medicine who has received requests for mentoring and many e-mailed requests to meet by people who have read some of her published work. These days, where many of us have a web presence, it has been easy for everyone from prospective medical students to seasoned professionals to reach out to her. When I asked her about finding a mentor, she told me,

> I've seen a lot of people be very creative in this sphere. Of course it is great to have someone locally who can play this role for you,

but sometimes that just isn't an option. There are wonderful professional networks that people can tap into. Sometimes it is in their specialty. There are a lot of mentoring programs that are embedded in these professional societies. If you go to the annual meeting they will link you up with a mentor and get the conversation going that way. People have also created a relationship after seeing someone give a talk and they will e-mail them afterward and ask, "Can I sit and talk with you?" because he said something that resonates with me and the person thinks he or she might have something in common with them and that works.

She has been in the medical profession for about thirteen years, and she has had mentors who were nonclinicians and nonphysicians and their support and advice have been instrumental to her. She encourages physicians to reach beyond medicine for their mentors because their universe is much larger than just the people around them. "Don't be afraid to take the first step toward someone and don't be afraid to look outside of that comfort zone, whether it's your hospital, your practice, the profession of medicine, or your specialty, to find someone."

Doug Freeman, founder and CEO of Virtcom, has an A-list of corporations who attend his conferences and sign up for his management training sessions. As a former professional in the financial industry, he understands the value of doing your research about finding a mentor. In between planning one of his mega-diversity conferences, we had a chance to talk about some of his strategies for finding a mentor.

There are sponsors out there. We talk about oftentimes in the workplace that we are doing competitive intelligence and we're doing competitor analysis and marketplace analysis. But what about sponsor intelligence? Have you done your intelligence at work and homework to understand who the key sponsors in the organization are? If you have identified them, have you identified the pathways to which you can be interesting to that sponsor and engage a relationship with them? Have you prepared strategically for when you get the opportunity, whether it's on the elevator, whether it's at a company picnic, or whether it's at a sales meeting or a formal dinner? Do you have a game plan of what you're going to say to engage the person and build a relationship? What are you going to bring to the table?

With so much available in social media, you can start by looking at your potential mentor's LinkedIn page. Is the person a baseball fan? Does he or she go to church? It is almost like looking at this as a sales approach for an employee. It's taking those people who are excluding you and looking at their value proposition. Oftentimes we have to reengage and learn the value proposition of some of those people who may be unintentionally excluding us, give them some of the benefit of the doubt, and engage those people once we have strategized. You're not going to get everyone in that clique on board, but maybe you might get one or two people and they'll be the beginning of the process of inclusive network building. The key is being proactive and prepared, because nothing would be worse than mispronouncing a key leader's name or stumbling over your presentation when you approach this person. A lack of confidence and preparation could lead to a reputation and impression that will be difficult to overcome.

One of the greatest ways to find a mentor is to have that mentor find you. There is a direct correlation between the amount of positive buzz about you and your visibility. So how do you create positive buzz? One way is to say yes when you are invited to participate in or volunteer for a worthwhile project. Often, we think that we don't have the time to take on more committees, boards, and organizational work. However, Linda Gadsby, legal counsel for Scholastic, Inc., has a litmus test for determining the value of a project: her teenage son.

> I try to choose things that I think are going to be impactful. I try to balance it by not being out in a given week more than two nights because I like to be home so that I can—not do homework with my son anymore but—see the homework even if I don't necessarily completely understand it at this stage. I like to see it. I like to pretend that I know what he's doing. And also, just to be there to talk. So I try not to be out more than just a couple of nights a week.

I try to pick activities that I think when he looks at how I'm spending my time, he will get it. He will say, "Yeah, that was something important that my mom was doing. I understand why she wasn't home that night with me." That is one of the barometers that I use.

When we ran into each other at the New York Links Gala and caught up on each other's lives, she explained why she balances it all. "The real reason you should get involved is that if someone has taken the time to identify you as someone that they want to work with or to be involved with a particular project and they are seeing something in you that they think is valuable or they want to expose you to a group of people that you haven't had exposure to or who haven't had exposure to you." She was offered the opportunity to serve on the Board of the NYU Law Alumni Association immediately after she transitioned off of the Minority Law Alumni Association at NYU. Although she was ready take a break, she thought about the fact that this was an opportunity to have access to a group of alumni that her previous role didn't offer—the broader law alumni group of active alumni. This service activity would also give her greater exposure to administrators at the law school, and would also position her as someone who is interested not only in activities or issues that are important to alumni of color but also those issues that were more broadly important to alumni of the law school. So she decided to accept the opportunity. Saying "yes" opened a number of unexpected doors for Linda.

In 2013, when the law school was looking for a new dean, one of the five people the chair of the selection committee asked to participate in this interview process was Linda. At the time that the chair called and asked her to participate, she was on the road going to Ithaca, New York, to put on a conference for a group of 300 women at Cornell, another organization that she led. She would have had to commit to a pretty short turnaround to participate in this interview process. The thoughts going through her mind included the many things she had on her plate. But, she thought about the fact that it was a great opportunity; a high-level opportunity; and there were a number of people in that alumni board that the chair could have asked to participate in this process but he decided to ask her.

I think about the fact that sometimes when people step out of their comfort zones to ask someone who is not perhaps their natural choice to ask—it's not their buddy and it's not someone who works at their firm—it takes a little bit more effort for them to ask someone different who is not in their circle. We should accept that olive branch that's being offered. I accepted the opportunity to participate in that interview process for the dean. Had I said I was too busy to do this law alumni association, I just came off of this other leadership opportunity and I'm not going to do this, I would have never been in the position for these other majority alums to get to know me, to get to know my skills and capacities such that I would've been in this position to interview for the new dean of the law school. It's not that you always have to say yes, but if you pick opportunities well, they can lead you to relationships that can be helpful to you down the line.

When you notice that you are not invited to join an informal mentoring relationship, you should ask yourself what you are doing to attract a mentor. In addition to proving yourself professionally, are you proving yourself altruistically? If you are looking for someone to take time out of his or her business schedule to help you, you too have a responsibility to help others. The *each one teach* theme constantly came up as I spoke to professionals about whom they have chosen to mentor. During a Martin Luther King Humanitarian Award ceremony, I lucked out when I shared the stage with former *Essence* editor Michaela Angela Davis. She is a huge proponent of girls supporting other girls. "I got my mentor when I was on my way professionally. That's why I try to get my mentees when they're young like in college, and I make sure that the mentees in college are mentoring people in high school. That's the deal with me. If you want me to be a mentor, you have to be a mentor."

Rhonda Joy-McLean, who you will read more about in the chapter about managing bullies, often advises mentees that they are not empty vessels for her to fill.

Mentors are often concerned about how they are spending their time and whether or not they're helping the mentee. From the mentee or protégé's point of view, when they reach out to their mentor they need to understand that their mentor is probably very busy. Just because you don't hear from them doesn't mean that they don't care. It usually means that they are swamped. Try to find something that they are interested in and send it to them. I'm interested in cooking, traveling, and reading, and I'm always delighted when one of my law students—I run the law internship program at Time Inc.—will contact me and say, "I heard about X and thought that you might be interested," and they will send it. So I encourage mentees to think about the relationship as going both ways.

However, there is a fine line between being aggressive and being assertive. Michaela understood the value of being persistent without being a pest. "I stalked one of my mentors because I really needed to know what she did." Michaela wanted to get to know Beth Ann Hardison, who had a successful modeling agency. She was a Black woman in the fashion industry, an industry that is notorious for lacking racial diversity. Michaela would sit on the stoop of her brownstone with a cup of coffee for Beth. "I just really went in hard because I needed to know her story because I felt like I was trying to get somewhere that I haven't seen anyone else do." However, Michaela advises that you have to take the temperature of the person. For some people, Michaela might have seemed obnoxious, but twenty-four years later Beth Ann is still her mentor. What kept Michaela out of the annoying realm was constantly asking herself before approaching Ms. Hardison, "Is there anything that I can do to make her life easier?" Throughout her career, Michaela has been able to attract some of the most incredible women to mentor her. "Susan Taylor just kind of picked me up when I was really, really new. We have to swoop each other up. Susan was in a place where she could do that. A lot of times women don't feel that there are places where we can swoop up that other girl, or because it took us so long to get to this place we are very insecure about embracing another girl. It is so important that when we are in some place safe and stable and in a position of power that we go and get a girl or young woman."

During your self-introspection about the state of your mentoring relationships, you should also consider your reputation. Ascunsion "Sunny" Hostin, legal analyst for CNN and a former big law firm associate, shared her views about the importance of reputation because all if not most decisions about your career occur when you are not in the room. "Often when someone cannot find a mentor, it is because of spotty performance or not having the right word on the street about you." Getting someone to mentor you is a matter of one's political capital. "For mentors of color and women, our political capital is so difficult to come by, so we are protective of our political capital mostly because it's difficult to help anyone else after a squandered opportunity. For example, if you recommend someone for an opportunity and they disappoint, you ruined the capital that you could use to help other people. It's unfortunate when this happens because you're a little bit more reluctant to help the next time and do a lot more due diligence." It is also important to be realistic about your work environment as you see mentors. "The television world is different, especially since it is so competitive. Unfortunately, there's room for only one morning show anchor or only one evening anchor. So, when you're looking for a mentor you are seen as trying to take that person's job."

If you are having difficulty finding mentoring support in your office, poke around at the offerings by professional trade organizations. The American Association of Advertising Agencies (AAAA) is a good example of an external initiative to build an internal pipeline. The advertising industry is known for its paltry numbers in racial diversity. According to Bureau of Labor Statistics data from January 2008, the advertising field—defined as advertising and public relations agencies, as well as media, direct mail, and other operations exclusively devoted to creating and delivering ads—is just 5 percent African American, 3 percent Asian, and 8 percent Hispanic or Latino. Those numbers are particularly stark considering that New York—the city with the highest concentration of ad agencies—is only 45 percent White, according to US Census data. Advertising is an embattled industry that in 2006 was the subject of a New York City Commission on Human Rights (NYCCHR) investigation involving sixteen prominent New York firms, including BBDO, DDB, Ogilvy & Mather, Saatchi & Saatchi, and Young & Rubicam. In response, the AAAA bolstered its diversity efforts. To help its member advertising firms, the AAAA's Multicultural Advertising Internship Program (MAIP) helps to provide soft skills to college undergraduate and graduate students who are presented to the advertising industry at the end of every summer as a unique pool of candidates ready for hire. The interns are given a lot of training that will help them to self-manage their relationships and manage their expectations. An important component of that is understanding how to reach out to someone who can be an informal mentor, present yourself and your need, and make it easier for that prospective mentor to take you on. It is helping young people to understand how to initiate a conversation. By giving them the tools and the language to use to spark the conversation and to be interesting as mentees to a prospective mentor, MAIP works to put them miles ahead because they go into their new situation in the agency ready and excited to experience the give-and-take that comes from an informal mentoring relationship with the supervisor. Receiving the type of information that MAIP provides the mentees, the supervisor will hear a conversation that says, "I'll make it easy for you to mentor me. Here are some of the things that I need, and here is what I will do with the support that you give me as a mentor. I'm not going to be a time burden on you, but you will be important to my development and here's how I will further support this relationship as I continue as a young person or mentee growing in the organization."

Singleton Beato, executive vice president of Diversity & Inclusion and Talent Development for AAAA, is the heart and drive behind MAIP's success. When I asked her about the lack of ethnic diversity in advertising, she explained to me, "We do not have opportunities to cultivate mentoring in our agencies. We work in breakneck speeds all the time. We are out there servicing clients, and we don't spend enough time helping our managers of people and our leaders of people understand the importance of guiding and facilitating discussion between themselves and those that require some informal mentoring. It's a challenge." The MAIP program turned forty years old in 2013 and has an incredible network of 2,400 alumni. One of the challenges that the advertising agencies have is making sure that they have multicultural people at the senior level. The MAIP alumni network satisfies the need for junior-level people to see, experience, and develop relationships with people of color who are senior to them, even though they may not be in their same ad agency; they are a part of an extended family. Through the MAIP program, AAAA brings them together in different places in different parts of the country so that they can share an experience and feel that they have a space that has been created just for them. These are lifelines that are unique to people of color that help to keep them in the industry and feeling inspired and respected.

Career development is a two-way street, and it is your responsibility to be proactive about getting what you want. It is a good idea to be courageous and let people know that you want their help. Sometimes you have to lead someone's hand in your direction to get them to help you. When you go to them for help and ask for their advice, people generally feel honored and will share valuable information with you. If you appear sincere and humble in your approach, more people may reach out to you.

As the employee, how do you get brought into the loop? An August 16, 2005, *New York Times* article, "Have You Heard? Gossip Turns Out to Serve a Purpose," underscored the importance of gathering crucial information about the workplace by using office banter to your advantage. The article proposes that "When two or more people huddle to share inside information about another person who is absent, they are often spreading important news, and enacting a mutually protective ritual that may have evolved from early grooming behaviors." Stay in the loop and speak to colleagues to find out who within the organization is good at mentoring and is willing to make connections for others. But remember to keep a safe distance from too much office gossip. You want to stay in the loop and not get tangled in it.

Lisa Charles might have benefited from talking to her colleagues about their relationships with partners. If she learned which partners were reaching out to associates, she might have been able to make herself more available to them.

Remember, your mentors do not necessarily have to look like you. Alexis Thomas,* an African American woman, would never have made it through her first job in college without Jessica Siegel, a White Jewish woman.

I interned for a magazine and Jessica was the editor who basically adopted me as her office-child. She not only taught me about the administrative workings of the office, but she also taught me about the little things that I didn't understand about networking within the company. She explained the importance of going to social functions, especially the company holiday party. She took the time to explain the magazine business to me. She left me in charge of manning a display table at an exposition when she had to go out of town. She even introduced me to the Internet. (Yes, this was quite a few years ago.) At the time, I took her kindness for granted and just assumed that all bosses were hands on. (Doesn't it seem like we had the best bosses earlier in life?)

I actually looked forward to going to work each day because I knew that someone, Jessica, cared about my well-being. I cared about doing the best job possible, and this was difficult. I wrote about computers and really technical, stiff, and educational products. I was nineteen years old and I wanted to write for this new hip-hop magazine called *Vibe*. Although I was bored out of my mind reading about the latest Microsoft products, the last thing I wanted to do was disappoint Jessica. During my twelve-week summer internship, there was only one day that I did not report to work and that was due to a railroad strike. At the time, I didn't even think of the word "mentoring," but that's exactly what she did for me. In return for Jessica caring about my career, she earned my loyalty.

Sometimes we forget to use all of our resources, from the secretary to a senior executive. People who have been with the organization for any length of time know the personality layout of your office and can advise you as to who is more affable and who is not. When you find a mentor, it's not necessary to call him or her a mentor. Some people get overwhelmed by titles and feel pressured to perform. To avoid the risk of someone shying away from helping you, just flow with the relationship. And most important, ask for help. When people know that you want to be mentored, the caring ones will work with you.

Here are some other strategies and approaches that professionals have used to move from outsider to insider.

Taking Charge: A White Woman Partner in Her Late Thirties Shares Her Strategy for Finding a Mentor

I have never really felt like an outsider in the workplace. I came to my firm because my former firm really did not have many women. So I knew that that was important for me, and I wanted to work for and with a woman who was a rainmaker or whatever you want to call it. When I came to the firm, that person became my mentor and has always made sure, from my perspective, that I got the same work as everyone else and that I am accepted in every way. The mentoring has been very important, but the other thing is if I ever felt that I was not getting the same opportunities as someone else, I've always been very vocal about demanding what I think I'm entitled to. So, if a case came along and I thought that I was the right person, I stood up and said that I was the appropriate person. With one partner in particular, that style works best with him. Once, a case came in and he was talking to me about it, or I had overheard him discussing who should staff it. I knew that it was going to be a high-profile case. I simply went to him and gave him my pitch as to why I was the appropriate person. And, I think whether I was the appropriate person or not really didn't matter. He was more impressed that I came forward and said I think I'm the right person.

When I approach a partner, I am super prepared. I find that that is another thing that makes sure that you get the right work. As long as before you talk to someone you are super prepared, you have done the research, you've thought about your talking points and about what message you need to get across, you'll get the work.

It's All about Confidence: A Latino Ivy League Graduate Discusses His Insights for Leveling the Playing Field

I was fortunate enough to work in different environments where I was not subjected to bias. Oftentimes I was the "first" within the respective groups to be a person of color and have a decent pedigree. So, I really didn't face exclusion. However, being in the executive search world, I hear from a lot of individuals that I provide counsel to that those challenges are clearly out there.

The mind-set really predicates the behaviors. I didn't walk into the environments thinking that I was going to be subjected to any form of bias. I was confident in what I was able to bring to the table. There are always challenges, but not challenges based on race or gender, but more so knowledge share. Behaviors are crucial in the marketplace. I provide counsel to many individuals. I would have to say that people have, and I wouldn't say a lack of self-esteem, but a lack of entitlement. Why they hired me really is not predicated upon quotas or diversity programs, but more so they hired me because I am a qualified individual. So entering into any type of work environment, I know stepping into it that I was entitled to take on a specific role and while I was confident in my own self, I think that I was able to project this outward. So those types of behaviors were not only being a risk taker and being proactive, but I think feeling a sense of confidence being myself and knowing that I can deliver. It sets the foundation. There are those who tend to be a little weak or meek and tend to be susceptible to attacks, whether they're founded or unfounded. There are those who always claim that they're a victim and within those who feel victimized there is a further dichotomy: those who are qualified, meaning those who are high performers, and those who are not high performers. So the question becomes, is the feeling of marginalization justifiable or not. So that's a separate issue unto itself.

The advice I would give to individuals who may feel like Rudolph, that they don't get to play in any reindeer games: I would suggest that they get to know the political landscape. They have to be confident in who they are and what they bring to the table. If you're not going to be able to toot your horn, have others who will toot your horn. And be surrounded by individuals who are a good reflection of yourself. Find the mentor who is out there to help navigate the landmines that are in the corporate landscape. There is no magic bullet that provides the individual with that sense of comfort, but there are many tools that they can utilize to help minimize the phenomena of marginalization by virtue of your ethnicity or gender.

MENTORING TURNOFFS

Many times we don't know why someone we have reached out to has stopped returning our e-mails or taking our telephone calls. Here are some of the mentoring turnoffs that people have shared with me:

Professor Katherine Milkman (Wharton School of Business)

I was actually on a panel recently with a group of other academics talking about mentoring doctoral students in part because of my research on the topic of how faculty respond to doctoral students seeking guidance and mentoring, and we were asked a similar question. What are mistakes doctoral students make that turn off advisors? One that I think is really maybe underappreciated is over-asking. And I don't just mean in terms of time commitment. I think one of the best things a mentor can do for a mentee is to expand their social network by connecting them with others: bringing them to lunches and dinners with other senior-level executives at the firm or other important faculty members. I think one thing that is particularly a big turnoff for mentors is when a mentee explicitly requests to be brought along to an event where the mentor may, for instance, not feel comfortable bringing someone at their level. So those kinds of big social asks feel like a natural request from a mentee and can be a big turnoff for the mentor.

A self-invitation to a dinner with faculty, for instance, from a doctoral student at a conference can be awkward to deal with. So that's one. Generally, over-asking for time is tough. Recognizing that the mentor you're seeking a relationship with is extremely busy and overcommitted is important, and it is probably related to how they became successful enough to be a sought-after mentor. You have to be very careful in terms of how much of their time you request and figure out that balance between over-asking and not getting enough value out of the relationship. Particularly, focus on "am I asking something that could make this other person feel uncomfortable because I would be the only person who is this junior attending this event—if I'm asking to attend an event—or I'm asking this person to spend an inordinate amount of time with me given their other time constraints?" So trying to get some sense of whether you're making an appropriate request, and making typical requests may be something you can do in part by asking other people who are in mentoring relationships, "Have you ever asked this of your mentor? Is this a typical thing to expect?"

Asuncion "Sunny" Hostin (CNN Legal Analyst)

You have to be the architect of your own destiny. I hate when people say that they were iced out of this opportunity or that opportunity. You have to make your own way.

Melody Barnes (Former Senior White House Advisor to President Obama)

Some people can be relentless. They aren't seeking a thoughtful, constructive interaction; they are really using you as a crutch and trying to avoid doing the hard work necessary to grow and advance professionally. You have to think about what you're asking of a person because it takes time out of their day and because they are managing their relationships as well. If you're hearing "no," then accept that you're being told "no, I can't do that, but I can do this for you." I think some of it is about being sensitive to your mentors as well. I know I keep that in mind today as I seek advice and support from others.

Michaela Angela Davis (Former Essence Editor)

The sense of wanting to be big and bad and not wanting to do the work and be self-starting. It's a turnoff when a mentee has the same problem over and over and does not actively work on it. Self-pity is a turnoff. Not looking at where you can help is a turnoff. It's really important for me to see that the person whom I mentor has a sense of service and a sense of sisterhood. I've had to let people go or they just naturally fall off. When I was at *Vibe* I had an intern who hadn't been there for long. She had this idea that she could skip the steps because I was her mentor. She wanted to take the elevator, not the steps. You grow from taking the steps.

Singleton Beato (AAAA)

A big turnoff is if you have a mentee that doesn't seem very engaged in the process of learning and growing and working hard. I have a great example of the ideal mentor-mentee relationship. There is a highly successful professional at one of the large advertising agencies who took on an intern even though he really had no time to do so. What ended up happening was that they cultivated a relationship whereby he not only mentored her but he also helped her to become one of the most successful people in the agency at a junior level because he said that she worked hard and anything that he asked her to do, she did. She seemed very eager to prove herself worthy of the time that he was giving her as a mentor. He said, "I was inspired and excited to watch her develop and grow."

If you have mentees who are very invested in themselves and in their career and they demonstrate to a mentor that they are going to do positive things with the experience or knowledge that is provided to them, then that is exciting. If you have a mentee who is laid-back and lazy and does not want to do the work and wants you to spoon feed them everything, that is a turnoff. If you have mentees who do not know what they want to get out of the relationship, they are not asking questions, they are not leaning in, that is a turnoff. If they do not follow through with what they say they are going to do, like showing up for a mentor-mentee meeting on time, or not following through on an assignment that is given to them by their mentor, these are turnoffs. People who are not responsible, who do not seem to be engaged and ready to do the hard work, that is a turnoff. You demonstrate in your behavior as well as in your communication that the time that is being invested in you is well spent and appreciated, and that it will be utilized effectively.

CHAPTER TAKEAWAYS
- Mentors are attracted to people who believe in mentoring others.
- When people feel overlooked, they stop investing in the organization.
- When seeking advice and guidance, be ready to implement the advice and guidance that a mentor invests in you.
- Professional trade organizations can provide the mentoring that might be missing in your workplace.
- Mentoring relationships have boundaries, and it is a good idea to share notes with your colleagues as to how they are staying within the respectful boundaries with their mentors.

CHAPTER 2
RECOVERING FROM MISTAKES

As hard as we may try, we often fall short of the glory of being perfect. In line with the theme "Failure is not in the falling down but how you get up," how we recover is greatly affected and determined by those who are on the receiving end of our mistakes and have the power to forgive. People in the out-groups are often led to believe by our parents and our supportive communities that we have to be twice as good as our majority counterparts because people are expecting us to fail.

These theories about double standards partly grow out of the observation that people in the majority are often forgiven much sooner than people in the minority. Let's use Mark Rich as an example. This billionaire financier was indicted for evading more than $48 million in taxes and charged with running illegal oil deals. He received a pardon from President Bill Clinton and today lives comfortably in Switzerland.

Even in the court of public opinion, offensive White radio personalities are quickly forgiven for their antics by other White men. During the 2007 Don Imus fiasco where he called members of the Rutgers women's basketball team "nappy-headed hos," Republican and Democratic presidential candidates, respectively, Senators John McCain and Christopher Dodd condemned his actions but then quickly issued their forgiveness and even agreed to make future appearances on his show, which fortunately was cancelled.

Yet, minorities, African Americans in particular, have a much harder time making a comeback. How many of you remember—or even know of—Janet Cooke? Ms. Cooke was a *Washington Post* journalist who won a Pulitzer Prize for a story about an eight-year-old heroin addict, and she was later exposed as a fraud for concocting the story. Her punishment started with rightfully stripping her of the award, but the public and the journalism community never forgave her. She disappeared from public life and was never able to recover from her mistake. During an interview with NBC almost ten years after the incident, Ms. Cooke was clearly unforgiven for her mistake. Ms. Cooke was working as a salesperson in a retail clothing store, and the interviewer commented that her inability to ever work in journalism and her permanent fall from public life were what she deserved.

The Reverend Al Sharpton is another example of America's good memory when it comes to what they perceive as mistakes minorities make. Rev. Sharpton's credibility is still questioned twenty years after supporting Tawana Brawley, a Black teenager who accused White law enforcement officers of sexual assault, which many thought was a hoax. During a 2007 broadcast, MSNBC's David Gregory did not hesitate to mention Rev. Sharpton's involvement with the scandal in the context of discussing Don Imus's racist and sexist comments. Interestingly, today, Rev. Sharpton has his own show on MSNBC, making he and David Gregory cable mates.

As people in the minority, we watch how the double standard of performance and forgiveness plays out and we do not expect anything different in the workplace. When our colleagues in the majority make mistakes, they are forgiven and put on the path to redemption. We see how our colleagues in the majority sometimes get extra coaching and attention from managers and consultants to brush up on their skills. Yet when we make similar mistakes, if we do not have someone from the majority invested in our success, it is almost impossible to ever make a comeback.

Although we all make mistakes, how we're dealt with makes all the difference. Are you given a second chance or are you forever marked as the careless employee?

Tanesha Pierre* understands what it is like to not have an opportunity to come back from a mistake. Tanesha is a Haitian woman who graduated from a second-tier law school and landed a position as an associate at a first-tier corporate law firm in New York City. Although she worked tirelessly to churn out quality work, she found that people were more willing to work around her as opposed to with her.

I had instances where I submitted an assignment and I was told that what I handed in was not specifically what was asked for. My work was not to someone's liking. Instead of the person giving me back the assignment and outlining what was wrong or right, explaining what should have been done and what was required, I was basically told, "I'll do it myself or I'll have someone else do it," rather than showing me how to do it right the first or second time around. Whereas my Caucasian counterparts and classmates were mentored and reviewed the assignment line by line as to how it should be done the next time. They were given second opportunities to do additional work where I was not.

Usually these encounters were with senior associates, but in one instance this occurred with a partner. I gave her an assignment that she requested. She never got back to me. I asked her numerous times if she had any comments on the document that I produced. If there were any comments, please let me know. I never heard from her. I decided to check the status of the document in the firm's shared folder on the computer system and I saw that the document was totally redone by someone else and I was never told why my work was wrong or how it should have been done differently. So apparently that partner didn't feel that she should have come and spoken to me about how she wanted the assignment. She either did it herself or had someone else do it and never got back to me or told me, "this is the proper way to do it." So I never had the opportunity to learn from my mistake.

This experience made me feel pretty inferior. It made me feel as though my contribution to the firm was not appreciated or valued and that the work environment is not nurturing and mentoring to a minority like myself. So I really felt like I was not given the opportunity that my Caucasian counterparts have to really learn and hone and shape the skills that I need as an attorney.

Tanesha was cheated of the opportunity to correct her substantive work mistakes. Her managers and superiors did not inform her of her mistakes earlier in her career at the firm and instead misled her into thinking that she was doing well. One by one, partners and senior associates did not want to work with her. Eventually, Tanesha, who was once deemed valuable by the firm, was branded as incompetent after six years and was asked to leave. Fortunately, another firm saw Tanesha's talents and scooped her up immediately. She is now in a more nurturing environment where her managers value her contributions and do not overlook what she has to offer the firm.

Sometimes the hardest mistakes to recover from involve what we said or did in a tense situation. How many times do you wish that you had a time machine to go back in time to retract a comment? Most of us have been in situations where we wished that we reacted differently. People in the minority sometimes find that their faux pas are not so quickly forgotten or forgiven.

Wade Tong* is a young television reporter of color who learned a lesson in double standards when he tried to advocate for himself.

One particular ratings period, my boss said, "Hey, I want you to do the morning show." That would have required me coming into the studio, doing the morning show, and then anchoring my show at 11:30 and then leave at noon. Well, I did it on and off to fill in during the ratings period, but I didn't like it. That's not what I was hired to do. I was hired to work 9-5, Monday through Saturday. I like to anchor my show and then go out and find stories for the afternoon show. I filled in several times and I never complained. That's my policy. No matter what happens, I just go in. I've never called in sick; I never miss a day of work. I'm always there at my time slot. If I'm supposed to be there at 9 A.M., I'm there by 8:30 A.M. every day.

Then one day on the set, one of my co-anchors asked me, "Hey, are you going to be the permanent morning show reporter?" I said I hope not. That's not what I came here to do. I was bothered by this arrangement, so I went to my news director and maybe I handled it the wrong way but I said, "I didn't really come here to be a morning show reporter. I came here to anchor the mid-day news. I was in a small market in the Midwest. If I wanted to do a morning show I would have gone to Atlanta or Chicago to be a reporter. I'm a little concerned." The news director said, "You know, I have a plan for the morning show but I'm not going to tell anybody what it is yet. I told you that I just need you to do the morning show temporarily." I finished out my time on the morning show.

When it was time to renegotiate my contract, during my review, my news director brought the situation back up. He said, "One thing that really bothered me is that you came to me with this 'big anchor' ego, like 'I didn't leave Cincinnati to do your little morning show.'" Now that is not what I said at all. In fact, I just said that I was concerned. My news director said, "Well, to me it was like you were too good for our morning show." I told him that I disagreed with him because from the day I was hired, anytime the station called me, I would even jump out of bed in the middle of the night and go cover stories about fires, shootings, or whatever. The news director said, "I'm not going to renew your contract. We're just going to go month to month because I just don't feel like you want to be here and I don't want anybody here who doesn't want to be here." That really, really upset me. I thought about it and thought maybe I should take responsibility for it. Maybe I brought this on myself. Maybe I didn't handle things the right way because I try not to complain.

The news director eventually hired someone for the morning show to be a flat-out morning show reporter. However, while he was looking for a morning show person, he changed my co-anchors. He tried out at least three women at the anchor desk. He put an Asian woman with me at the anchor desk and I thought that she did very well. I thought she had energy, personality, we got along well. In fact, we're friends so it's easy. I thought she did a good job. He brought in this person who is his favorite, a White girl, and said, "I have an opportunity for you. You can do the morning show and then anchor the 11:30 news." She said, "I don't know if I want to do that because I don't want to be a morning show reporter." He said, "But you have this great opportunity to anchor the 11:30 news." Her response was, "I'm concerned because when I leave here I want to leave here as a reporter/anchor. If I do the morning show I would be limiting myself to doing live shots." He got mad at her and said, "Don't expect any favors from me." When I heard about this, I thought maybe he is fair. The news director was upset with her and opened up the offer to do the morning show to everyone else.

He eventually gave the anchor position to that White woman. I just assumed that she apologized to the news director and asked for another chance. But, she and I were in the make-up room getting ready and she goes, "When the news director first came to me, he said that he had a great opportunity for me and I told him that I didn't want to do it. And then the news director said, 'Well, I don't want to have two reporters anchoring a show and then trying to turn stories on short deadlines.'" She said that she initially turned the morning show down and then after two weeks of having the Asian woman anchor, the news director called her into his office and said, "Do it for me. Just try it. If you don't like it then don't do it." I thought, that's funny, when it was me, he told me that I had this huge anchor ego.

The double standard in forgiveness is most apparent in the disciplinary scheme. There are times when a supervisor will give one employee some slack when he messes up. He may bend the rules for an employee who shows up to work late because the employee is usually punctual or is a top performer. A boss may decide to overlook an employee's workplace infractions because they have developed a personal relationship and a boss does not want to come down hard on his friend.

The ability to overlook one employee's infractions over another's has the detrimental effect of marginalizing the employee who watches others receive preferential treatment. While an employer may be instilling good employer-employee relations with one employee, he is potentially ostracizing the employee he chooses to penalize. When employees in the minority notice that they are the employees who are treated by the book while their majority counterparts are not, this creates an environment that says that discriminatory discipline is a part of the unwritten rules of the workplace.

Raheem Mohammad,* a television executive in his thirties, remembers when he was reprimanded more harshly than his White female counterpart for the same offense.

There was an incident where I was severely reprimanded by my direct report for what he called a dereliction of duty when we were at a regional convention in Newport, Rhode Island, and I took this person I was dating with me. She ended up being around for the first day of the show. My supervisor wrote me up and said that I was being detrimental to the company; that I was representing the cable network, and this is something that he didn't ever want to see again. He came within two sentences of saying, "I'm going to have to let you go." I took that very seriously. For me, it was extremely hurtful because I didn't think that I did anything that was detrimental to my work. However, in the evening I did take time to be with my girlfriend. And that's really where his point was. According to my supervisor, I was on call twenty-four hours a day.

So, as it turns out, a couple of years later when I didn't have that territory anymore, a young lady who was Caucasian ended up going to one of the events at the same show with her then ex-husband. She did not want to go alone. The interesting thing was that she got the same speech from the same supervisor that I received, but she was not put on notice that she had ninety days to clean up her act. That was the only time in my work history that I felt that there could be discriminatory proceedings because why is it that I'm almost fired? Although I did not share the details of my reprimand, she shared her story with me. I asked her what was the outcome, and she said that the supervisor really laid into her and that she felt really bad. But what didn't happen was that she was not written up, and her position was not threatened. She was read the riot act and then everything was OK. I didn't quite understand the difference if it was the same dereliction of duties. Why didn't she receive the same level of admonishment from the senior person? That was the only time in my eighteen years that I was treated differently because I am a minority. They were both Caucasian and I was not. As it turns out, I was gone within three months after that whole incident.

ERADICATING THE BARRIER TO RECOVERING FROM MISTAKES

We all make mistakes and should acknowledge that no one is perfect. However, in our pursuit to impress clients and increase revenue, we are sometimes excessively harsh when employees make mistakes. Punishing an employee, eternally, for a small mistake is counterproductive to workplace harmony and performance.

For example, Kendra Washington* admits that she was unable to see past socio-economic status when managing a summer associate from a privileged background.

I'm about to reveal a major secret about attorneys—well, it's only a secret to those who have never worked in a law firm. Attorneys are some of the worst people-managers. For all our intelligence, and access to leadership training (some of us even hold MBAs in management), some of us still do not know how to effectively manage others, especially when it comes to giving feedback. I could never understand how some of the brightest legal minds did not provide constructive criticism and valuable guidance to their associates and staff. Instead, partners would send clandestine e-mails to other partners about an associate, or just flat out complain to anyone who would listen—even the clients. This was an inexplicable phenomenon to me until I managed my first summer associate.

I asked the summer associate to find a statute I needed for a writing assignment. That was the first and last substantive assignment I gave to her. I didn't give her too many details about the project because I assumed that what I needed was simple and self-explanatory. It was simple and self-explanatory because, of course, I understood what I needed. Circular reasoning is never a good thing, especially when giving assignments.

The summer associate was going into her third year of law school and had worked for the firm for two summers in a row. She was from a wealthy area of Connecticut and seemed smart enough to research a statute.

The next day she proudly walked into my office with a sheet of yellow paper torn off of a legal pad. She had written, or actually scrawled, the statute in red ink. I was speechless. I was so stunned that I could barely find the words to utter a polite "thank you." I didn't think that I would have to tell a law student (1) to type the information I needed, and (2) if it had to be written, not to use red ink!

A few days later, she asked me for feedback and I had tons. I was actually offended by her submission. I felt like *the help*. I didn't even read it. I tucked it away in my desk drawer, researched the issue myself, and went on with my day. In the days that followed, she would stop by my office asking for feedback. She desperately wanted to know if she did a good job and if I had the information I needed.

I suffered from the same problem that ails most managers. Often, we will not provide feedback unless we really care about a person's professional development. Honestly, I was so swamped with work that I didn't want to invest the time in the summer associate. I thought, if I have to tell this woman not to use red ink when completing assignments, she is too much work for me and I don't have the time.

In hindsight, I wish that I had managed the summer associate differently. I should have given her the opportunity to redeem herself. While my experiences (and common sense) taught me that red pen and handwritten briefs are unacceptable, I should have given the summer associate the opportunity to explain herself. Was the office out of black and blue pens? Did she not have access to a computer or word processor? Was she under a time crunch? This may have been the first time that anyone told her that red ink is not acceptable in the workplace. Now, if she made the same mistake again, then I would have been justified to move on, but without investing five minutes of feedback in this associate, I cost myself time and wasted a potentially valuable resource.

Kendra finally realized that if a candidate was good enough for the firm to hire, more likely than not the employee should be good enough to develop. Managers should try to create ways to develop their employees' skills and abilities. A manager may try to assign a point person to work closely with the employee who is perceived as underperforming. That person would be easily accessible to the employee to answer any questions or provide feedback on projects.

Underperforming employees often do not know exactly what the problem is with their work because managers do not take the time to explain the shortcomings. Managers should try to be as specific as possible when describing where the employee went wrong. If the employee turned in a writing assignment that was not to your standards, explain where the employee should try to improve. Was it a grammatical issue? Content? Organization? If so, zero in on the issue so that the employee has a clearer idea of what he or she should address.

For years, organizations have quietly given mediocre (and sometimes underperforming) employees coaching on everything from sales techniques to speech therapy. For instance, I know a law firm partner who invested heavily in a perky White woman who, as she described, "didn't know shit" when she was first hired. The partner invited the associate to her country home on the weekends, invited her to practice oral arguments in front of her husband—who was one of the best prosecutors in New York City—and continues to give her endless encouragement. Today that associate is on the firm's partnership track.

Not giving an employee in the out-group the opportunity to redeem himself can become an expensive practice for the organization. When a manager comes down hard on outsiders in the workplace for making a mistake while making allowances for other employees, these outsiders start to question whether they are working for the right organization. These employees may feel less valuable to the organization and as a result decide to leave. Patience is not only a virtue but also a cost-saver.

Honesty and fairness, theoretically, are two of the most simple—but realistically most difficult to implement—characteristics to guide managers through decision-making. When managers make choices based on what is right, they make it more difficult for employees to make accusations of unfairness. Employees sometimes know when they are required to jump through extra hoops to get the same treatment their colleagues in the majority get; people talk. When employees in the minority notice that they are penalized more harshly than their majority counterparts for similar conduct, it ruins office morale and, if egregious enough, may lead to a lawsuit for disparate treatment. When disciplining employees, ask yourself, are you following company policy for one employee and not the other? Does the punishment for a person in the minority exceed your usual office protocol, even though you are following the written company policy? Are you scrutinizing one employee instead of another because of your personal preferences? If the answers to these questions are "yes," then you may potentially open up your organization to lawsuits.

When people feel as though they have been treated unfairly, they look for justice. Under federal and most state antidiscrimination statutes, employers are prohibited from subjecting an employee to disparate rights and privileges based on protected characteristics—race, age, disability, national origin, gender, religion, and color. Employers are sometimes successful in defending discrimination claims where employees were not similarly treated; companies waste thousands (sometimes millions) of dollars defending an action that carried the stench of discrimination. Is office favoritism worth a trip to the Equal Employment Opportunity Commission?

OVERCOMING THE BARRIER TO RECOVERING FROM MISTAKES

If it has not happened already, there will come a day that you will make a mistake at work and may even be reprimanded. Some employers understand that for any number of reasons your work will not always be perfect. This may have been your first assignment and you did not completely understand what was being asked of you. Or, you may have had an off day and missed an important deadline. In reality, you will make mistakes, buy you can void being a repeat offender. While you should strive to be the best at whatever you do, you also want to have a plan for recovering, quickly, from a mishap. Try to admit and understand the mistake, make a note of it (if necessary), and move on. Dwelling on mistakes does nothing but create unnecessary stress. Our society is built on the backs of survivors who did not allow their mistakes to hamper their success and moved on.

(Just think of Martha Stewart after Imclone, Janet Jackson after the Super Bowl wardrobe malfunction, or Sean "P. Diddy" Combs after the New Year's Eve shootout where he was charged with illegal weapons possession.)

Be sure to own up to mistakes without over-apologizing. Most managers do not have the patience to hear someone continually say "I'm sorry." It gets annoying and makes you look wimpy. Most managers just want to know that the employee understands what he or she did wrong and intends to remedy the situation.

As an outsider we are hyper-visible, and often more self-conscious about our mistakes. I truly appreciated Keith Boykin's candor and vulnerability when I spoke with him about recovering from mistakes. It was difficult to imagine this confident CNBC anchor ever having moments of doubt. As you can see from the picture he painted of his days in politics, he almost called it quits because of a small mistake.

I think everybody makes mistakes, and I think the problem that we often fall into is that we think that that's the end of us. My philosophy is that the only difference between people who are successful and people who are not is that people who are successful don't give up when they fail. Because everyone fails. The example I can think of which is really, really petty but symbolic was when I was working my first campaign when I was in college.

My job was to follow the candidate, and the candidate was Governor Michael Dukakis, on the campaign trail. One day I was supposed to be on the airplane and get to the aviation terminal. I got there a little early and no one else was there. So I said, "Oh, I have time to go and take care of some other things." So I left the general aviation terminal in my car and drove to the main terminal to get a razor because I didn't shave that morning. I thought I'd be able to make it back in time. If you've ever been to Logan Airport in Boston, it is a little confusing.

As I was driving out from the main terminal to the general aviation terminal, I took a wrong turn and ended up going back to the tunnel back to Boston, and I got stuck in traffic and I wound up getting back to the airport much later than I was supposed to. I delayed the entire flight; they could not leave without me because I carried this little metal suitcase that's called the multsoc, which the media needed in order to plug into the candidate's speeches whenever he was going somewhere. They could not leave without me. It was so embarrassing. I let down the campaign. The reporters were waiting. The governor was waiting. All the staff were waiting. I felt like I should fall on my sword. The press secretary yelled and screamed at me when I got out of the car at the airport. My first instinct was to resign because I let down the governor. He looked at me like I was crazy and asked why would I do that?

One of my informal mentors, Deborah John, who was an African American press secretary for the campaign, she was on the plane that day as well and she had a fear of flying, so whenever we flew she would literally hold my hand over taking off and landing and she told me that day you can't give up, you have to keep doing what you have to do. You can't resign or quit over something like this. That day I learned something important. You cannot let your mistakes define you, and you have to have people in your corner to help you out and mentor you.

Contrition is an underappreciated virtue, and far too often when we make mistakes we have a tendency to become defensive and to explain instead of to apologize. I think that my apology, my sincerity, and my willingness to be honest and to promise to not make that mistake again was appreciated. And they knew I was a good person. They knew I was not trying to do anything malicious. It wasn't a part of my character to do something like that. You are not your job. I'm learning every day about the power of reinvention.

My interview with Dacia Toll, founder of Achievement First, which has twenty-two charter schools throughout the Northeast, to discuss recovering from mistakes was off to a rocky start. While I was en route to one of her schools, she called to tell me, "I don't think that I'll be of any help to your book." While she is aware that there are real barriers in the world to inclusion and access for women, she didn't feel that she has personally encountered that many, partly because she has effectively been an entrepreneur. Since graduating from Yale University and being a Rhodes Scholar, she has not worked in traditional workplaces. However, I insisted on the interview because this is the type of attitude that predicates success. At the core of Achievement First is a belief in "results without excuses." Following Jim Collins's theory of the Stockdale Paradox, her organization always confronts the brutal fact of whatever the reality is and maintains an unwavering faith that it will prevail in the end. Although most of Achievement First's schools are ranked among the highest in their states, she admits that two of her twenty-two schools are struggling.

> It's important to claim that and say this is reality, but I have incredible faith and optimism because we meet challenges and we go after them. We make mistakes and we fix them. We fall short, we get our tails back up, and we go after it again. Stronger and smarter. That's probably one of the number-one skills that we are trying to develop in a first-generation college educated student. It's what we call grit. There is this research at the University of Pennsylvania that says grit out-predicts IQ in terms of success in life. That ability to get your tail back up and go back at it is profound. So what we're trying to teach our kids is what we try to model. When I make mistakes, and I make plenty of them, or fall short, the only way for me to feel better is to go back at the challenge to fix it.

Remember to have faith and confidence in your abilities. We all make mistakes, and it is important to remember that everyone has had a setback or two. Do you recall President Bill Clinton's nomination speech at the 1988 Democratic convention? I'm sure he hopes that you don't. His speech was long-winded, tedious, and boring. In Washington DC's political circles, that speech—when people remember it—is known as the worst speech ever given at a convention. Did President Clinton disappear after this setback? Of course not. President Clinton learned from that experience, won the Democratic party's nomination for president in 1992, and has perfected his speaking abilities to the point where he is now known as one of the best communicators in the world. Today, he earns upwards of $250,000 per speech.

CHAPTER TAKEAWAYS

- The double standard in forgiveness is most apparent in the disciplinary scheme.
- The ability to overlook one employee's infractions over another's has the detrimental effect of marginalizing the employee who watches others receive preferential treatment.
- Not giving an employee in the out-group the opportunity to redeem himself can become an expensive practice for the organization.
- Our ability to forgive may greatly depend on the extent of the biases we possess toward members of an out-group.

CHAPTER 3
MANAGING BULLIES

At the risk of stating the obvious, no one likes to be yelled at and humiliated in the workplace. In 2006, a Wharton doctoral student and professor conducted a study about respect and its relationship to burnout in the workplace. In *What Makes the Job Tough? The Influence of Organizational Respect on Burnout in Human Services*, the researchers explained that "Respect is a way in which employees get entrenched into the workplace and feel that what they do is meaningful."[37]

Yellers, throwers, and people who steal credit for your work are nothing but bullies. Bullying in the workplace is on the rise and is gaining recognition as a national and international problem. According to a study conducted by CareerBuilder.com in 2012, 35 percent (an increase of 27 percent since the previous year) of US employees say that they have been bullied by a coworker, manager, or customer.[38] A quick Web search about bullying yielded websites like mytoxicboss.com, bullyingonline. org, and bullybusters.org. There are even institutes that specialize in helping employees to deal with bullies. A *New York Times* article, "Fear in the Workplace: The Bullying Boss," found that some people bully for the "sheer pleasure of exercising power," while others do it to "swat down a threatening subordinate."[39] Regardless of the motivation, bullying can affect the target's health, self-esteem, and feelings of engagement.

Indiya Harris* dealt with passive-aggressive bullies every day when she practiced law for a mid-sized firm in New York City. While her superiors rarely raised their voices, their nitpicking and needling of her work was their way of asserting control. Indiya recalls an incident in her firm that made her question how much longer she was going to be a bullying partner's victim.

> This one instance that I can think of clearly, I was working on a case and the partner and I went to the client's place of business to

47

interview an employee. This employee was adverse to our client. During the course of the interview, I could see that my partner did not like my being there as a Black person and as a woman. During the course of the interview, he had me there and I was asking questions, but when he wanted me to go off the record he would ask me to step out of the room. We were a team and we were supposed to work together. This partner didn't trust me. It was an age discrimination case and I felt that he assumed that because I was a woman, Black, and member of a minority group, I would sympathize with the plaintiff more than I would sympathize with our client. From the beginning, that was my feeling. The plaintiff was a White man. We were doing an investigation, and I felt that the investigation should be a thorough investigation. The investigation he was doing was a whitewash.

Our client wanted the investigation to come out one way, and the partner was doing everything in his power to see that it came out that way. Instead of doing a regular investigation where you look at all the facts and then you make a determination at the end, the partner had his conclusion and he was trying to put the facts to the conclusion. So, every time there would be a question or an instance that our client may be liable or may be a wrongdoer, he would ask me to step out of the room. I just did as he asked because I felt that one, he was going to take me off the case, which he did eventually, and two, I couldn't question him in front of the client and if I asked him to step out of the room with me, he wouldn't have done it so there was nothing for me to do.

I felt frustrated and angry. This did not affect my work product, but it did affect the partner's work product because he became super critical of me. Things got out of control when he didn't even trust me to write up the investigation notes. For instance, I interviewed an employee who used the word "seconded," which he defined as he was working for a law firm and the law firm loaned him out to our client—who was at that time a client of that law firm. I took for granted that the definition was right because it sounded right. We were asking him pro forma questions, you know, nothing substantive.

You know, warm-up questions that you would ask like, "when did you start at the firm, when did you finish." So this guy's answer was, "Before I was hired as a full-time employee, I was *seconded* from the years blah blah blah." And we asked him what was seconded, what did that mean? I was in charge of writing up the notes, and I put in the word "seconded" and explained his definition as a footnote. I did it for two reasons: one, when I went on the Internet and looked up the definition it seemed similar and the word usage seemed consistent, and two, it wasn't a big deal. Well, when the partner got it he sent me an e-mail asking me if I looked it up in Webster's dictionary, and why didn't I put the definition in the notes. It was clearly his way of bullying. And that's the word, bullying me, trying to get me to take myself off the case. I felt like an outsider because I was the only African American female with children in the firm. You were looked upon as untrustworthy. That is the word, untrustworthy. They cannot trust your writing, they cannot trust your analysis, they cannot trust your not sympathizing with the "other side." They don't trust you or want you to be there.

Not too long after that incident, Indiya decided that she was too smart and too good of an attorney to work in an environment where she was bullied. After hoarding away enough of her $200,000 a year salary, she left the firm to open up her own practice.

While I have never been threatened with a hurling stapler or any other piece of office equipment, I have seen and heard of all types of abuse in the workplace. In fifteen years of working—from a high school job at a local hospital to working in law firms—I have overheard vicious arguments where people used more expletives than nouns. Yet, I have never seen anything productive accomplished by such physical and verbal aggression.

LaTanya Smith* became the victim of old-fashioned bullying early in life. She was a college freshman and quickly learned that not all adults act like grown-ups.

My mother hated my first job when I was in college. It was a part-time job with my college's campus dining services. "Dining services!" she would exclaim. "I didn't send you to school to wash dishes, clean other people's floors, or cook other students' food." Actually, I worked in the administrative office and helped students with their meal card dilemmas. Although I never washed a dish or stepped foot in the cafeteria's kitchen, all my mother could envision was me cleaning trays. Similar to most ambitious West Indian parents, she was a proud woman who wanted nothing but the best for me. She was concerned about the caliber of people I would work for in "the kitchen." After my first and only year on the job, I would agree that she had good reason to be concerned.

Campus dining definitely was not the type of job with an extensive career track. Most of the student workers did a nine-month stint during the academic year and moved on. There was no succession planning or training for new employees. For the first six months, I was left on my own to figure out the office's procedures and processes. My boss was a lazy woman who mostly used me to get her coffee (with sixteen packets of sugar) and cookies from the dining hall rather than helping her with necessary filing, typing, and other clerical work. She had stacks of untouched papers on her desk; she was a mess.

At the end of each month, the office filed its accounts receivables statement with the main office. Well, one month my supervisor could not find the statement. When I walked into the office, my supervisor's boss—who outweighed me by one hundred pounds and was at least fifteen years older than me—pulled me by the collar, demanding, "Where is the statement?" She had a menacing smile on her face and thought she was being funny. In her twisted mind, she probably thought she was just joking around. I was not laughing. I was scared. I couldn't believe that this woman, an older woman who signed my paycheck, thought she had license to physically grab me. (If I knew then what I know now, I would have reported her to the dean and the president's office. Based on that stunt, I'm sure that the university would have given me a complimentary lifetime meal plan to keep the incident quiet.)

Instead, I took a less political route. I spoke to the next senior person in the office, my supervisor's boss's boss, who realized that

I was upset by the incident and apologized. In the middle of my sheepish and inarticulate retelling of the events, I let it be known that I would not stand for abuse. I didn't know what would happen if I complained, but I knew I had to. I could not continue to work for campus dining and keep in my feelings of disgust and humiliation about the situation.

When I told my mother about the incident, she thought I overreacted. She thought that my boss was being playful by pulling me by the collar like the "tough guys" do in the movies. My mother and I just didn't see eye to eye. Even though my mom was no big fan of the job, there were benefits that she couldn't deny. I had flexible hours, a complimentary meal plan, and lived within walking distance. She feared that I would lose my job. Fortunately, my boss's boss was understanding and agreed with my assessment of the situation. While no immediate action was taken, I like to think that my complaint had something to do with my lazy supervisor getting fired by the end of the academic school year. By the way, she later found the missing document on her desk, trapped underneath a pile of other documents I'm sure she thought an office intern lost.

LaTanya's encounter with the micro-inequity of bullying due to her age was unsettling, but even more curious was her mother's reaction. Given that LaTanya's mother never even wanted her to work for campus dining, I was surprised that her mother did not support her decision to report the situation. In search of an explanation that would help make sense of LaTanya's mother's perception of the collar incident, I spoke to Bruce Tulgan. Bruce Tulgan is an expert on generational differences and the author of *Managing Generation X*, among many other books. During our conversation he explained the stark differences between how boomers and my generation react to aggressive behavior from our bosses.

Generation X has a much different point of view about their employment relationships. The older generations were told keep your mouth shut, do what you're told, wait for your boss to notice you, and wait for the long-term rewards to vest. With Gen. X and Y it's today, tomorrow, next week. Any kind of abusive behavior—forget discrimination on the basis of an impermissible classification or reason—is not tolerated. If you don't like the way I dress, too bad. Bye! You throw a stapler at me when you're frustrated? There are all kinds of things that people used to tolerate that Gen. X and Y won't tolerate because relationships in the workplace are more short-term and transactional. The younger and least experienced people start out assuming short-term and transactional, so they'll just go work somewhere else. That's another factor beyond just the expectation. You could be shocked that you are being discriminated against and then say this is going to be a drag if I'm going to be here a long time.

Shirley Pelosi* was in her twenties when she determined that if she did not confront the office yeller, each day at work would have been a drag. For seven years, Shirley was director of marketing and business development for an architecture firm in New York City. The firm was sixty-six years old. It had been started by the father of one of the partners. There were seven equity partners, and they ranged in age from forties to seventy-five. They were all men. When she attended partnership meetings, it was she and seven guys.

From the moment Shirley started working for the firm she was ambitious. The firm's partners wanted her to do a marketing plan and a marketing budget, which she had never done before. Shirley figured out the ropes on her own. However, her efforts were often overlooked.

I never really let myself get too intimidated by it, but there were moments. The partners would gang up on me and say, "You don't get it. You're not an architect." Although I was the only nonlicensed professional in the room, I didn't let it get to me. During meetings when they would ask, "Why are you doing this? Why, why, why?" I had to really know my stuff and stick to my guns. I couldn't let it get in the way of doing my job. It was a triumph. They started to respect my recommendations regarding which projects to accept and reject.

One of the partners was a yeller, and his idea of communicating was yelling. The yeller would walk into my office, shout at me, and then walk back to his office. It scared the hell out of me, getting yelled at by a guy my dad's age. I told him, if you want me to work here, you cannot yell at me. You cannot treat me like a child. That won his respect.

Eventually, I left the firm due to a lot of infighting between the partners.

ERADICATING THE MICRO-INEQUITY OF BULLYING

While managers are in a powerful position and can, technically, exert their frustrations on employees by belittling them in front of their coworkers, these employers will not win any loyalty contests with their employees, especially when the bullying is motivated by demographic differences. Managers should consider the long-range effects of their emotional outbursts and think twice about how they talk to people. Are you raising your voice? Are you speaking to your employee the way in which you would want someone to speak to your daughter or son? Is your aggressive behavior really going to accomplish anything?

Governor Malloy of Connecticut does not tolerate bullies and recommends that employers get rid of them as soon as they are identified. Before becoming the governor, he was Mayor of Stamford, and before that he practiced law for twelve years in a small, general practice law firm. He is well acquainted with how bullies operate. "There are certainly bullies in law firms. Some of them sit on the bench, some of them are prosecutors, and some of them are attorneys."As an executive, he is aware that bullies try to hide their behavior from him while instilling fear in their workforce. That is why he encourages managers to create an environment where bullies cannot hide. He wants to empower his employees to come forward and report any boorish or belligerent behavior. "When I was mayor if I saw that, we have a term *a person needed to be taken to lunch*, and that meant that that person needed to go. Sometimes you don't learn about a bully as quickly as you'd hope you could."

There are usually other attendant problems. Not only does aggressive behavior in the workplace have the potential to reduce your employees' productivity, it sometimes comes with an expensive price tag. In 2006, the National Education Association paid $750,000 to settle a sex discrimination lawsuit that was based on one tyrannical employee's bad behavior.[40] A high-level male supervisor subjected his female employees to yelling, screaming, and profanity-laced verbal attacks. The EEOC described the supervisor as "turning bright red with bulging neck veins as he screamed, coming so close [to the women that] they often felt his saliva spit on their faces." Although the supervisor's harassment was not sexual, the court of appeals did not dismiss the case on the grounds that "harassing conduct does not have to be motivated by lust or blatant misogyny to be illegal sex discrimination."

As you can see, there are serious consequences for hostile behavior in the workplace.

OVERCOMING THE MICRO-INEQUITY OF BULLYING

Bullies in general are not discriminating based on protected classes. They would not have gotten as far as they may have if they only targeted women and minorities because women and minorities aren't the only people in the workplace.

Bullies tend to seek out whoever they feel has vulnerabilities: people who have a history of not speaking up or newly hired people who may not feel that they have earned their stripes yet. (Why should people listen to them? They don't have a ton of experience that others have.) Many times employees in the nondominant out-group—age, race, gender, national origin—are among the most recent hires and they may have fewer instances where their intelligence and their worth have been demonstrated to others. It's not that bullies are only targeting out-groups, but that the bullies tend to seek out opportunities where they feel that people in general are not going to be that strong or they are not going to push back.

For some, bullying is just a personality trait, and they bully others wherever they are: restaurants, soccer fields, and pretty much any setting. Others tend to target when they feel that there's a chance to acquire power or exercise it in their workplace or places where it's useful to them.

Sometimes, dealing with a bully requires the same strategies used on the playground in elementary school. While your workplace bully is not the same as your school bully, who employed peer pressure, verbal abuse, and humiliation, the workplace bully is similarly overpowering and tries to get his or her way by usurping all of the power base. Remember when the playground bully was tamed? It was because someone stood up to him or her. The same concept often applies to bully bosses. Once you shock a bully by responding and checking his or her behavior, the bully will think twice before doing it again.

Diane Yu, co-founder of the National Asian Pacific American Bar Association and deputy president and executive director of the Sheikh Mohamed bin Zayed Scholars Program at New York University, offered some great advice for managing bullies, given that she has dealt with some throughout her career.

> Based on the literature I've read and my experiences, the only real survival technique is to choose carefully but pick an issue where you will take on the person and challenge their point of view. You take on a bully with good allies and good evidence and good support. You don't take them on lightly because the bully is practically a professional at knowing how to shut down dissenting views. You have to be sure that you have something worth saying, something worth advocating, and something worth arguing, and you must be able to do it twice as effectively without being disrespectful. You cannot allow yourself to cave in and be unable to speak up. It's very tough.
>
> Sometimes women, people of color, or any individual who feels that they are not fully trusted or accepted, or who feels that they are at the receiving end of bullying, will find it difficult to stand up. That's what a bully wants. Studies have shown that the only people that bullies respect are the ones who take them on. You have to be prepared and you cannot be naïve about it. It takes patience, strategy, planning, and practice. Once you do it, it gets a little better the next time. While you can always stay quiet, I don't think passive-aggressive people are helpful to the organization or the employer because you don't know what their issues are until it is way too late. Any possible constructive or helpful alternatives that they could have proposed are lost. It's very damaging to the organization when bullies are allowed to proliferate and get their way

because it chills any other people with good ideas but who lack courage, strategies, or support. It takes guts and it can be uncomfortable.

If you're doing this for the first time, take on the bully in an area where you feel very knowledgeable. Often when a bully sees that he or she is outnumbered or the quality of argument is so superior to whatever they're recommending, they sometimes will back down and you don't have to have a huge fight. Many times bullies are smart and not usually dumb. If you size up the situation and strategize and find allies for your position who address different parts of the argument, your strategy becomes quite powerful. Then the rest of the group can say, "Now we have our cover; now we have our information and persuasive reasons as to why we can go in a different direction." It's a leadership challenge.

Ironically, bullies are often the kind of people that no one is happy working with, so they often, and eventually, get sabotaged by poor reviews or less than enthusiastic reference letters when they are trying to take another job or move to a different department. Sometimes the lack of interpersonal skills comes back to bite them.

Rhonda Joy-McLean, deputy general counsel for Time Warner, told me about her run-in with a bullying boss who eventually got what he deserved.

You need to pick your battles. Sometimes you have no choice but to respond because the conduct is criminal. There are times when you must take action to protect yourself and others. More often than not, inappropriate conduct falls into a murky area. You need to ask yourself, "Can I still do my work?" For me it's all about work credibility. Once, one of my former bosses responded to an e-mail in a very rude way. I had sent what I thought was very good e-mail advising the client, and I copied my boss just as a courtesy. My boss was known for sending these 3 A.M. bullets from hell. On Monday morning at 8 A.M. when I opened my e-mail, I saw the scathing response to my e-mail indicating that I was very unprofessional and that this was an example of how I was not supposed to communicate. That was one of the worst e-mails I've ever received, especially to be admonished by copying the client when my boss didn't really know much about the situation. If I had responded immediately with the e-mail I had in mind, I would have been fired right on the spot. So I made sure to talk to other people who also had experiences dealing with this individual. This experience taught me that you need to take time to consider how best to respond to a difficult and painful challenge. By the way, he eventually wound up getting fired because he did a lot of other things wrong.

John Rose is one of Connecticut's pioneering attorneys of color. He came from a family of twelve children, attended Dartmouth for college, and then Yale University for law school. In 1968, he was the first African American associate at an all-White law firm in New Haven. Today he is the backbone of the Lawyer's Collaborative for Diversity, which seeks to increase the number of attorneys and partners of color in Connecticut law firms. (As of 2013, you can count on one hand the number of equity partners of color in large Connecticut law firms.) Early in his career, he tried cases all over the city before he went to a private law firm. As he describes it, he was often the only "spot" in the entire building. When I asked him about his earlier days of practicing law, he described it as "an experience." He went on to tell me,

> When you're the only one, you work your tail off. We worked all the time; we were always ready. When we went to argue a motion in a criminal case, the case was dead because we had all the law. We had all the facts and we weren't afraid to try cases. Sometimes when I would try cases in a courtroom where I was "the only one," the judge tried to push me around. After practicing law for forty-seven years you learn that a judge is nothing but a man or woman in a pair of pants or skirt. So, when they push you around, you push right back. (When you're in chambers you cannot be held in contempt of court.)

However, standing up to a bully, especially if he or she is your boss, is not easy. There are reasonable and rational concerns that you will be retaliated against or even fired. Natasha Cormen* was a new attorney when she was blindsided by a bullying boss.

When Natasha looks back at a situation, she wonders whether she did the right thing.

Although there were many times where I felt like my work with this employment law enforcement agency was an oxymoron, things really hit rock bottom when I was yelled at for conducting research about a potential case. A Black woman came into our office to file a discrimination complaint, claiming that the security guards in her local grocery store followed her around the store because of her race. When I described the situation to my supervisor, his immediate reaction was, "Well if she's not doing anything wrong, then she shouldn't be worried about people following her." He was a White Irish man and he could not appreciate the humiliation a person of color could feel when they were treated like a criminal while doing something as simple as food shopping. So, instead of explaining my emotional feelings with him, I decided to conduct some preliminary research on the issue, that is, whether being profiled as a shoplifter because of one's race and being followed around the store could qualify as discriminatory conduct. I wrote a brief memo supporting my instincts and I left it on his desk.

During a weekly staff meeting, he threw the memo on the conference table and arrogantly snarled, "I got your little memo and it's not worth the paper it's written on. I just hate to think about how much time you wasted on that crap." (Now, we did not bill our hours, so there was no real concern about lost time.) Although I had research to support my position, he was not convinced. My fellow coworkers and I were floored when he said, "Even in a perfect world, if a security guard admitted that he was following a customer because she was Black, that's still not discriminatory." My research clearly showed that racial profiling was discriminatory. There I was just trying to do my job, and be conscientious about it. I could not believe how he publicly berated me.

The day after this incident, his tune changed and all of a sudden he demanded a full investigation of the complaint. He wanted undercover testers to visit the store location ASAP. You see, the head of the entire agency—a Black woman—ordered him to conduct a full investigation when she learned about his statements and conduct.

While I felt vindicated by the agency head's decision to investigate the complaint, I did not say anything to the supervisor who humiliated me and I will always regret that. I was too afraid to confront the supervisor because I was afraid that he would retaliate against me. But in reality, how could he have retaliated against me? He was already making my life miserable by embarrassing me in front of my coworkers. Looking back, I should have told him that yelling at me was unacceptable and explained how belittling my work was counterproductive. My silence told this supervisor that it was OK to yell at me and treat me like the rug he wiped his feet on. I took a passive-aggressive approach and just stopped caring about the agency and just tried to find an escape route out of there. I started to really "waste time" in the office by taking extended lunch breaks and taking every Friday off to find another job.

Natasha might have greatly benefited if she had discussed the bullying incident with a close colleague in a similar profession. Her internal cost-benefit analysis that she conducted denied her of valuable advice and feedback for handling the situation. She didn't allow anyone into the conversation in her head, and was left with many unanswered questions.

Jana Stephens* uses a drastically different approach when she feels like she is being bullied. Jana is a single mother with a young son. Not only does she think about her own career when she makes a decision in the workplace, but she also has to keep her son in mind. Jana has witnessed enough skirmishes in the workplace to understand that there are ways of fighting unfairness in the workplace without looking as though you are fighting.

There was an incident in a past law firm involving a female paralegal. She was on a business trip with a lawyer and they were at a hotel. She was in the hotel bar reading a book and the lawyer started talking to her. When she went up to her room, he followed her and tried to invite himself into her room. She came back and told me this. It was clearly inappropriate. But had she reported the lawyer to the firm, I don't know what action the firm would have taken and I don't know how far it would have gone. Her attitude was, "Why bother? It's not going to be helpful to me in my career. The incident has passed, I got through it, and it's not worth it for me to make a big deal." That's really the question, when to draw the line between filing a formal complaint versus getting through these things and chalking them up to boorish behavior. You have to admire people who are willing to file lawsuits, especially women traders in investment banks. It's really extraordinary that they do it, and a lot of times there's a lot of money at stake. In terms of them being known in the industry as the person who filed a complaint, it may or may not be where you want to be career wise.

Some high-stress environments like law firms and stock market trading floors are breeding grounds for aggressive bosses and coworkers. Some people just tough it out because they feel that misconduct is a part of the office culture and will just grin and bear it. Your response will greatly depend on how you much you love the work and need the job, as well as your threshold for working in stressful environments.

Although there are no federal laws against bullying, a workplace may have a policy to address hostile, harassing, or threatening behavior. As with any other issue in the workplace, check your employee handbook.

CHAPTER TAKEAWAYS

- It's not that bullies are only targeting out-groups, but that the bullies tend to seek out opportunities where they feel that people in general are not going to be that strong or they're not going to push back.
- Regardless of the motivation, bullying can affect the target's health, self-esteem, and feelings of engagement. Bullying in the workplace is on the rise and is gaining recognition as a national and international problem.

- While managers are in a powerful position and can, technically, exert their frustrations on employees by belittling them in front of their coworkers, these employers will not win any loyalty contests with their employees, especially when the bullying is motivated by demographic differences.
- Managers should create an environment where bullies cannot hide.
- Often when a bully sees that he or she is outnumbered or the quality of argument is so superior to whatever they're recommending, they sometimes will back down and you don't have to have a huge fight.

CHAPTER 4
SELF-FULFILLING PROPHECIES (PERCEIVED UNDERPERFORMANCE)

When Carolina Lopez* spoke with me to discuss the types of behaviors that ushered her out of her first law firm, the experience sounded like it was still a fresh memory. Carolina's resilience in the face of being undervalued for her contributions was an experience that only the strong could survive.

In my prior employment with a big New York firm with a small Los Angeles office, I felt excluded. It's hard to tell you the exact reason, but I'm convinced it was because I was young, I was female, and Latina.

I was assigned to work with a particular partner and a mid-level associate. They had a team approach on some of their matters, and in this particular situation that's what happened. The partner and I got along really well to the point where I think that the mid-level associate felt a little bit uncomfortable and threatened or something. I don't know what it was. She was a White female. The partner was a White male. He was a little bit older, and she was older than I was. (She came to the law as a second career.) I had done some pretty good work and had gotten some good feedback. We were working on something and I got excluded from discussions between the partner and the mid-level associate on a matter I was intimately involved in and had done a lot of the work on. Then, I had done a written assignment and was specifically told that she wanted to meet with me and give me feedback where she

63

then proceeded to lambaste me, indicating that I didn't know how to write. This really happened. She told me that I didn't know how to write, that I didn't know how to grammatically put together a correct sentence, and that she was convinced that I learned to write English as a second language.

This was the most humiliating, embarrassing moment that I could ever imagine, and shortly afterward it prompted me to leave the firm. I did end up talking to the partner about this particular project. His view of my work was completely and dramatically different. So, it was one of those experiences where I'm convinced that she acted the way she acted, number one, because of my gender and also because she knew about my ethnic background. She proceeded to try to press buttons that would maybe resonate with me or make me feel that I was not worthy or competent. Questioning my ability to write English—it was just an incredible experience. To this day when I've run into her at court, I can barely look at her. She knows full well what happened. I have to be honest; it really affected my self-esteem for a little while. What was crazy was that I had gotten some wonderful feedback prior to and subsequent to the incident from the partner. So I knew that I didn't have trouble with my writing or anything. It was really just an attempt to make me think that I was inadequate or maybe to try to get rid of me. I don't know. I couldn't tell you exactly what was going on. The experience is still fresh in my mind. I started to question even the basics.

The whole experience was incredibly negative, but I think I got some good out of it in realizing that I need to take ownership and mentor, especially women of color, which is what I've been very committed to in the profession over the last several years. I'm the hiring partner for my firm. Every mentee that I've had has been a woman of color. I've hired mostly women, but not all. I've increased our numbers and our racial and ethnic diversity in the firm. What I'm saying is that this event, but not just this event but my life experiences, prompted me to take steps to try to prevent this from happening in my immediate world in the future.

Nathan Jones* never had to wonder what his superiors thought about him; they blatantly told him that they didn't think that he would be much more than a good basketball player. Nathan, an African American man in his twenties, joined the military a few years after the army's advertising campaign of "Be all that you can be." He comes from a hardworking family from North Carolina and he had the potential of being the first in his family to even consider college. Unfortunately, his unfamiliarity with the college application and financial aid process convinced him that he could not afford college. That's when he turned to the US Navy. He entered a competitive engineering program and was determined to make the most of his military career.

Soon after he joined this elite program, he quickly learned that the military was integrated but not yet equal.

One instance where I felt like an outsider was in the military when my superiors made an obvious attempt to get rid of me because of my race. In the nuclear power program, while you were often tested, there were not many instances where one's knowledge was tested outside of scheduled tests. These instances—Academic Boards (ACs)—were dreaded by the students and reserved for those who had demonstrated a real deficiency. All of a sudden, the officers came up with an opportunity to randomly test five students' knowledge of where they were in the program. The day before the test, it somehow became a test of one person's knowledge. Me. When I was chosen for the AC there was one other Black guy in my class of thirty people; initially he was also *randomly* selected to take the test.

Before taking the test, I had to spend time interviewing with the officer who had set this whole thing in place. The officer made it clear in our interview that he thought that I would not pass the test, and I disagreed with him. He explained that people such as me did not belong in the program. He explained that people like me were better at other things, such as basketball and physical things. It was thinly veiled, but what he was referring to was still there. In an instance like that you feel like an outsider because it is being made clear to you that are an outsider. At the time, I was in prototype, which was the third phase to becoming a fully qualified nuclear operator. I was still in the training phase. There was nothing that I could think of that prompted the officers to test me. It started out supposedly as a random thing. If it was truly random, the decision to test five students could not have been prompted by anything the students had done. If we believe in the random quality of this decision to test, then it does not matter what I had or had not done anyway. It was just too coincidental how it went from completely random—testing five students—to selecting one person.

The other thing making it clear that there was an attempt to get rid of me was that when these AC are conducted, they were usually ten to thirty minutes in length. The majority of people who took them failed. The longest ACs were close to an hour. My AC board, which I would venture to say there is no record of, was eight hours long, which was the longest in the history of the program. An eight-hour AC board guaranteed you were going to fail. I didn't fail though. Although I had already qualified to be in the nuclear program, it's like they were giving me an extra test to see if I qualified to be in the program. You have to qualify to get to each stage in the program. At prototype you go through the in-class stage where they teach you everything you're supposed to know to get to the next stage, e.g., operation of the plant, in-hull. At that point if you show that you can't keep up, then they start testing you. There was nothing that I could have done to initiate their concern over my performance because I had not even completed the training. None of us should have been subjected to testing.

The way I operate—assuming that they really wanted to get rid of me because of my race—caused me to want to be there even more, specifically to do two things. One, to show that while you may think that people like me can't do, yes we can. And two, because of the constraints of the military and the way you can get back at people, I thought that this officer must be a racist, so my mission, as long as I was there, was to qualify for the next phase as early as possible, so that I could choose when I stood watch and find this officer and stand watch with him. I knew it would drive him crazy, which is what

I did. There was very little that I could do to him, but there's nothing that he could do to me once I qualified. He had to look at me every time we stood watch. It was the military, so I had to stay with the program. To get out of that program, one of two things usually happen, either you have a mental condition from the stress or you are going to be dishonorably discharged—you don't normally just switch programs; they have invested too much in you.

I did not re-enlist and I am no longer in the military. You can make a heck of a lot more money in nuclear power outside of the military and you don't have to deal with the same type of stress. Plus, as a Black man it is difficult to be in such a White program with such a White view and feel as though you can remain true to yourself. For me the decision to leave rested as much in my need not to feel dependent on the military as it did in the fact that I could not do as I had seen other Black men do: go along to get along.

Tammy Ellis* had a similar experience where her supervisor determined that she did not have the intellectual aptitude to do her job. Tammy is one of those people who thinks quickly and chooses her words very carefully. Whether she is in a conversation with her girlfriends or giving a presentation to attract a multimillion-dollar client, she is engaging. Although it is painfully obvious how eloquent and intelligent Tammy is, her employer could not see beyond her dark chocolate complexion to see how talented she is.

When I first started my practice after law school, I wanted to be a tax attorney. And for the first eight months of practice I was in the tax department in a large law firm. As I found out as I started practicing, the department that I was in was very typical of New York tax departments in that I was one of seven females in a twenty-three–person department. I was one of four non-Jews.

The bulk of the Jewish practitioners in the department were orthodox and male. That surprisingly turned out to be a very exclusionary experience for me in that oftentimes people spoke in Yiddish to my exclusion. There was very strong, reasonably so I guess—although uncomfortable to me—very pro-Israel sentiment and people were very willing to speak about their political and religious beliefs very freely, very openly, and with the assumption that everyone else in the room agreed. As one of the few non-Jews, I was always the one who didn't order the kosher meal where typically people who want kosher meals are the exception. For me, it was the complete opposite.

I also felt that that was the toughest professional experience because I also felt that I was targeted by one of the partners. I don't really know what his reasoning for it was, but much of his criticism was things like, "I don't think that you have the mental intellect to do this type of work," which was very surprising to me because I definitely have academic degrees and work experience that show otherwise. It was the first time that I had someone say to me, not that I didn't do a good job, but they didn't think that I had the ability to learn something, which was very disheartening and was very unjustified. And what substantiated to me that it was unjustified was that at one point I was working on a project with this partner and another partner. They were both supervising me. When I went to the partner who was very critical of me, he always had negative comments about what I was doing. And then I would go to the other partner, and he would say how excellent my work was and how much ahead of what he expected I would have done as a first year. So, it just seemed like such a dichotomy between the two opinions.

And even when the project was a presentation to be given to the department, I got tons of accolades from the people who attended the presentation, yet this partner refused to acknowledge that it was a well-reasoned, well-thought-out, provocative presentation for whatever reason. And so, being that he was a partner he made it very difficult for me because of course there would be partnership discussions and I was not there to defend myself, and he just made very negative comments about me to even the partners that I didn't work with.

While it could be said that maybe that's just the way he was with junior people, my officemate who was an orthodox Jewish male and junior in the firm was idolized by this partner. Even where we had very similar assignments where I got chastised for not knowing something, my officemate was taken under his wing. Even when my officemate made mistakes, the partner acted as though it was to be expected. My officemate got a lot of breaks and coddling that I did not get and I could not understand for what reason, other than the fact that I was not a Jewish male or someone that this partner felt comfortable with.

So towards the end I finally decided to leave the department because I refused to put myself through that situation any longer. Because I had good relationships with other people in the firm and other partners in the firm, I was able to get out of that department into the corporate department, where I was much more successful than I would have been had I continued to fight the system in the tax department.

ERADICATING THE BARRIER OF
SELF-FULFILLING PROPHECIES

In Greek mythology, Pygmalion loved his sculpture of a woman so much that it came to life. Oedipus fulfilled the oracle at Delphi's prophecy that he would kill his father and marry his mother. And, then there is Kevin Costner's character in the movie *Field of Dreams*, who was inspired to turn his farm into a baseball field when a voice told him, "If you build it, he will come." As humans, we are influenced to act based on our beliefs, which create our perceptions, which whether false or true, become reality. When we unconsciously believe that employees in the out-group are less skilled, less qualified, or less talented, we consciously look for affirmation of these beliefs. If we start a relationship from the premise that an employee is not going to succeed, more often than not, that employee will not succeed.

Similar to how work styles can obscure a manager's perceptions about an employee's abilities, visible characteristics can also distract managers from truly valuing the employee's work. Sometimes those in the minority might not be appreciated because their managers and coworkers are considering the *person* doing the work and not the *content*. When our subjective perception about how someone will work interferes with their objective performance, everyone loses. The employee perceived as under-performing constantly has to waste time fighting to defend his or her reputation, and the culprits risk ruining the organization's reputation for being a healthy and productive place to work. While I'm sure that some of the companies that appear in *Fortune* magazine's yearly list of the Top 100 Companies to Work For are led by managers who are real tyrants, I'm certain that the companies with a critical mass—and reputation—of employees complaining about bad bosses did not make the list.

OVERCOMING THE BARRIER OF PERCEIVED UNDERPERFORMANCE

When I practiced employment law, often my clients would have perfect hindsight 20/20 vision about issues that seemed trivial and snowballed into nightmares. They would tell me about the early stages of a plot to sabotage their career, yet they ignored the signs. They didn't take it too seriously when the manager strictly enforced the office's policies when it applied to them but then ignored the same policy when another employee was involved. They were the only person excessively criticized but receiving the least support and coaching. They had the most work piled on them. They did not get upset when a manager made a joke and comment that offended them. It was not until employees were fired or denied a bonus that they got upset and found meaning in these events.

Your work is your brand, and you cannot afford to have someone tarnish it. Too many times, my clients would present a file filled with positive evaluations but were still fired because someone did not like them for personal reasons and used workplace leverage to squeeze them out of the organization. The previous testimonials are clear examples of how managers' subjective and personal beliefs can taint the workplace dynamic. Tammy, Carolina, and Nathan were not people who objectively underperformed. They were commended for their work by some and admonished by others who were out to sabotage. Take note (or actually tons of notes for your records) when you feel that someone is unfairly disparaging your work or your performance.

Remember, people talk and you want everyone to say good things about you. Once you locate the source of the negative comments about your work, be sure to address that person and clear up any misperceptions about your performance. Maybe someone mistakenly thought that you missed a deadline when you were actually ahead of schedule. You should try to set things straight. Try to find the right time to address the source of the negative comments. Often speaking to this person alone and during a slower work period is more effective than addressing the person in a group during the office's busy season. If you are concerned about what you should say, practice your talking points with a trusted senior advisor. Remember to make the most of the people who care about your career.

When you get written accolades for your work, be sure to collect them. In your personal positive evaluations file, you should also keep any e-mails that you receive about your good work. Not only do positive e-mails cheer you up on those down days, they also create the record you may one day need to defend your work or file a complaint against the company.

CHAPTER TAKEAWAYS

- When our subjective perception about how someone will work interferes with their objective performance, everyone loses.
- Similar to how work styles can obscure a manager's perceptions about an employee's abilities, visible characteristics can also distract managers from truly valuing the employee's work.
- Take note (or actually tons of notes for your records) when you feel that someone is unfairly disparaging your work or your performance.

CHAPTER 5
FINESSING THE INSENSITIVE JOKE AND INSENSITIVE COMMENT

Sometimes insensitivity is caused by arrogance and a feeling that as management or people in the majority, it's good to be the king and that they can do or say as they please. In other instances, insensitivity is the result of ignorance and not knowing or being aware of how your words and actions offend the next person. In either situation, insensitivity still hurts. Insensitivity is not only the failure to care about others' feelings or circumstances but is also the lack of responsiveness. The person who ignores complaints of insensitive conduct is just as guilty as the person who makes the offending comment or gesture. The failure to do or say the right thing permeates all workplace relationships and fosters a culture in which insensitivity is acceptable. When a coworker or manager creates an environment that is uncomfortable or hostile, it just makes going to work more difficult. It becomes a draining experience to have someone belittle you and chip away at your self-esteem.

While cultural insensitivity is often taken seriously, callous behavior that is equally detrimental can take all shapes and forms. It could be fat jokes, unflattering comments about someone's color, or condescending statements about someone's socioeconomic background. Although the law maintains a "reasonable standard" and lists the protected categories for prohibited insensitive conduct, people are still offended regardless of whether or not the law prohibits the mistreatment.

Many of my consulting project assessments and trainings are around generational difference. The world is a much different place depending on the decade in which you came of age. For some, the Vietnam

War meant protests and tours overseas, while for others it meant really good films in the 1980s. It was not until Anita Hill's 1990s testimony that the term "sexual harassment" became a part of the everyday English language lexicon. And today, some young adults mistakenly think that the Cold War is a response to climate change. Out of curiosity, I decided to gather the stories about insensitivity through the generational difference lens. I wanted to directly compare baby boomers to Generations X and Y. When I spoke with baby boomers about whether they encountered insensitivity in the workplace, they all said yes; however, most did not realize it at the time. Many felt as though their majority counterparts did not really understand them and excused them for saying and doing stupid things. Others felt that insensitive banter was par for the course as a minority. As long as their jobs were secure, they did not get too upset about the "silly" things the guy in the cubicle next to them would say and do.

Jose Ramirez's* experience is a good example of how a boomer didn't even recognize how potentially detrimental jokes about his ethnicity were to his career and how he missed the signs that he was an outsider.

I've only had one time in my career that I felt like an outsider, and I didn't realize that I was feeling that way until I got much older and that particular part of my career was behind me. I am Hispanic and I realize now what was going on probably had to do with a bias. This happened earlier in my career. I had just gotten back from Vietnam, so that puts me in my mid-twenties. I worked for a company that was involved with mining. I felt that it was more that I was young or possibly I didn't have the right training or the right background. But then I realized that my peers, who were not much different than I was in terms of their backgrounds, seemingly were moving along professionally much quicker than I was. Their progress was better. I got to thinking about questions that bother me now but didn't bother me then. There was a guy who was in the position to promote me who would insert "humorous" jokes about me being Spanish. Again, I was born in this country. I come from a Cuban background. I wasn't thinking prejudice at that point. I wasn't thinking bias at that point. Now as I get older, I realize that that could have been the case.

Outsiders from Generations X and Y are much more astute at detecting and identifying insensitivity from their managers and coworkers. (This is probably because of the increased awareness about employee rights and responsibilities.) We realize that jokes are not just fun and play and tell a lot about what a person really feels. Going one step further, we understand that the same emotions that fueled a racist joke could also fuel the decision to deny us a promotion or even fire us.

In a sharp contrast to our parents, we not only recognize discrimination masked in insensitive conduct but we also take immediate action. Victor Chen* was known for laughing on the outside at insensitive Asian jokes, but his colleagues had no idea to what extent he strategized on the inside. Victor worked in the financial services industry for a few years after graduating from college, believing that there was real equality and equal opportunity. Instead, he met racism against Asians cloaked in frat boy humor.

Here's the interesting thing, one of my coworkers was being made fun of. He was Vietnamese and he had a somewhat striking resemblance (more or less) to Kobayashi, the hot dog-eating champion. His Asian-ness was used as a comical jump-off point for the predominantly Caucasian males in the group. His accent was also made fun of. It wasn't blatant like, "Oh, he's from Vietnam and he eats dogs." It was always like, "Oh, he has a funny accent. Look at the things he does. He's very thrifty." The composite of it was a very subtle, "Oh he's other. He's different. He's good at *that*, he's so focused." It was very subtle, like "Oh, this is what John* is good for." No one said that because he's Vietnamese he's this way, but it was almost like, and I perceived, that the message was, "John's never going to be a manager. He's really good at what he does and we really appreciate him for that." And I spoke about this with—aside from John—the other Asian-American male in my group. The conversations were very much about "they won't look out for us. We need to do what's best for us to get the best out of the situation." At the end of the day, our own self-interests were a priority while we were working there. We were finding a way to fit in, but knowing that we would never exactly fit in. I played the game.

I just worked really hard and I did a good job. I ascended to a place in that team where I did such a large volume of work and I had such a wide body of knowledge that I really became indispensable. So to me it became about work ethic and not worrying about marginalization. My goal was not to ascend and become a manager there. My goal was to get my bills paid and do some interesting work before I found the next big thing. When I found the better thing, I made the change to a career that I was more passionate about.

Victor's situation is typical. Managers and employees receive extensive compliance training and know how to avoid obvious and blatant acts of discrimination. However, just as quickly as in-group managers and coworkers have found subtle ways to marginalize out-group employees, these outsiders have found ways to decode their behavior.

Ironically, members of the majority sometimes feel as though they are in a "safe" environment when they are among their own, that is, they are safe to say whatever they think or feel about a minority group. In August 2013, an explosive video of Philadelphia Eagles receiver Riley Cooper calling a Black security guard the N-word became fodder for Sunday morning talk radio shows. According to The Institute for Diversity and Ethics in Sport (TIDES), located at the University of Central Florida (UCF), in 2010, 67 percent of the NFL's players were African American. Therefore, Riley's use of the derogatory racial slur was not uttered anywhere near an NFL game. It was said at a predominantly White Kenny Chesney concert. The apologies and tweets of support poured in after this video surfaced. However, there was still a question as to why he even used a word that would offend most of his teammates and players on other teams. Many wondered about dinner conversations at the Riley household. While members of a dominant group know their conduct may be offensive, many feel emboldened to engage in this behavior when there does not appear to be someone—especially someone from the targeted minority group—who would care. As we can see from Riley's situation, that is not always the case.

Heidi Williams, who is proud to be openly gay, found herself as that mistaken member of an out-group who was privy to the conversations of heterosexual in-group coworkers who did not realize that she was a lesbian. She repeatedly found herself in that uncomfortable situation where the people around her revealed their true thoughts and feelings about lesbians before they learned about her sexual orientation.

I can share some experiences I had when I was a flight attendant, which was an interesting job because you don't go to work with the same people everyday. Every other job experience I've had you develop a rapport and people get to know you. The airline industry is unique in that each time you go on a trip you could fly with different people and you could never fly with the same person twice. So you have to develop a relationship with people on each flight.

On trips, whether it was one day, two days, or five days of working with those same people, there were numerous times that I would be on a trip and be enjoying the flight attendants' company. We would talk about whatever things we had in common—what books we recently read, that we both were runners, anything. And it never occurred to me to bring up my sexual orientation. I'm a lesbian. They didn't bring up their sexual orientation so I would not bring up mine. It would not be something that I hid, but it just would not come up. Then when I thought I was really getting along with someone and had established a really good rapport, all of a sudden they would make a really homophobic comment. Unfortunately, I would feel really paralyzed. I think it was because it would catch me off guard. There was a time when I flew with a woman I just met. I was training for a marathon at the time and we happened to talk about how we were both runners, and we were talking about the books that we were reading. I really thought we were enjoying working together. On day three of this trip, she came and looked at me with disgust and said, "Oh my god, did you see how many dykes are on this flight?" It just took me off guard. I literally could not say anything. I think that whatever the stereotypes are I fit into the "normal" appearance for a woman, whatever that means. People assume that I am straight. They would share their prejudices and bigotry with me and think that I would agree with them, not realizing that I'm part of the group they're talking about.

When I was a flight attendant I would hear these negative remarks and I thought it was really interesting because my roommate who was also a flight attendant and was a gay man did not encounter the same degree of public homophobia. He was rather effeminate, and I believe that there is a stereotype that male flight attendants are gay and some of them are. I think that people didn't make comments around him because they just assumed.

I started to out myself before people could make the negative comments. I would put rainbow stickers on my name badge and on my bag. I certainly attempted to bring things up in a conversation as early as possible. Unfortunately, a lot of people don't know that the rainbow sticker stands for diversity and has been adopted as a symbol of gay pride and so it didn't always work. I think that at this point in life, I would feel disappointed in myself for not feeling like I immediately had the courage to say something back. I think over the years I've changed and attempted to immediately speak up so that I don't feel like so much of my power has been taken away. I'm really comfortable with and proud of who I am.

I actually got laid off after September 11th and by the time the airline called me back I had another career. It was really fun to fly around for four years for free, but I was ready for something more meaningful. I have moved on to a career as a full-time activist fighting for equality and I find this work extremely rewarding.

Although Heidi's coworkers thought they were safe to bash homosexuality when they were talking to her, they had no idea that they were offending her.

Regardless of the subtlety of the insensitive conduct, Generation Xers and Yers are quick to pick up when they are being marginalized. June Maples* was not naïve to her colleagues and superiors' erecting communication barriers to exclude her from conversations and business in general.

I did not share in the common ethnicity and culture of the majority of the department. I was a Black woman and I wasn't Jewish. I was outspoken, but a personable person in that I could carry on conversations with people in the department as well as with people outside of the department. Oftentimes during meetings—be they small meetings with two or three people where assignments were given or be they larger department meetings, people started talking about things in Yiddish in front of me. In my opinion it was just done purposely to exclude me because I don't speak Yiddish and I didn't understand what they were talking about. As a woman of Afro-Caribbean descent I could not become a part of these conversations and it became exclusionary.

When people are forced to internalize offensive comments and behavior in the workplace as a coping mechanism, it affects their ability to think and work productively.

Gem Winehouse,* an advertising sales representative for a global media company, spends unnecessary amounts of time thinking about what she says because of a mistake she made earlier in her career.

I was in a sales meeting of about ten people and I accidentally said "pacific" instead of "specific." My White female boss at the time said to me in front of the group, "We don't speak Ebonics at the office, we speak proper English." My colleagues gasped when our boss said this. Now, the California Ebonics debate was being covered at that time in the news, so my boss probably just labeled all Black speech as Ebonics or Black slang. However, I was still insulted and told my boss that my saying "pacific" instead of "specific" had nothing to do with Ebonics.

Gem was frustrated that her mistake was no longer an individual's mishap, but it was now an intrinsic aspect of her race because her boss determined that all Blacks speak Ebonics. This type of generalizing and negative stereotyping about employees does not go unnoticed.

Subash Singh* has had her fair share of feeling frustrated because of insensitive ethnic stereotypes.

There was an attorneys' meeting where one of the senior partners made a comment about people whose last names were not American, and specifically she enumerated that they were Chinese, Indian, and Korean last names. And, she made a comment about how these individuals, once they got their degrees from US colleges, were going to go back to their home countries. So that definitely was amazing to me because I have an Asian-sounding last name. I'm sitting across from the woman and am literally rendered invisible. On two levels it was troublesome: one, I wondered, "Is that how you think of me? A non-American or a foreigner?"

I've talked among my peers about it, but I have not directly confronted anyone who has said something or made me feel uncomfortable. I've talked to two other senior people about the foreigner comment and they agreed it was inappropriate and they couldn't believe it was said. Their reaction was she just didn't realize what she was saying, which does not justify the situation. These senior people asked if I wanted to speak to her about it. They tried to think of ways of addressing the issue, whether it involved me personally or other people stepping up and saying something. The fact that someone can't say your name I think automatically leads people to be kind of shy around you.

Sometimes insensitivity is not about what is said but about workplace decisions that result in minorities being assigned to controversial projects that are personally offensive.

Sharon Ross* tells an interesting story about how her law firm was oblivious to how its attorneys of color, and their allies, would react to the firm deciding to represent a company that once traded African slaves.

I worked for a firm that held itself out as a place that promoted diversity and had quite a few programs that on their face would benefit minorities. But then there was an instance where the firm allowed a particular racially charged case, a reparations case, to come in and assigned the case to a minority person and it caused a lot of uproar at the firm. I felt that I was excluded in that we, the associates of color, were never consulted with respect to that type of case. Had I been in the majority, that type of case would have never been brought to the firm. The firm's management said that they had been approached before about representing the Nazis but they chose not to because of what the Nazis did to the Jews, and so on. So they did not have any problems not representing the Nazis.

But in this case, because it was a client who had been sued for reparations, it didn't even occur to the firm that it would have been an issue for the racial minorities who worked for the firm and that the firm should have consulted us and taken our temperature to find out how we felt about it. I felt that because of the minority group I was in, being an associate of color, I was on the outside and I had no influence.

In fact, the firm's decision to accept this case led to a mass exodus of minority lawyers from the firm as a result. Considering that we didn't have that many Black people to begin with, over a period of time, six or seven and maybe ten Black attorneys left, and that's a lot considering that most firms don't even have that many.

The firm considered the numbers to be so significant that they brought in diversity consultants and begged the minority lawyers to not take any action until the firm had all these meetings to discuss the issue. It had not occurred to the firm before that Black attorneys would leave when the firm accepted a reparations case. You would think that it would have occurred to them because there was a minority partner who was in charge of the gate keeping. I guess she was asleep at the wheel at the time. She claimed that she was busy and didn't have a chance to look at the reparations case. In essence, I feel that since the firm held itself out as promoting diversity and having all these programs that favor minorities that this should never have happened. The only reason why it happened was because the aggrieved party was a minority. It just was not as significant for the firm to lose a huge client.

To be honest, I was torn. I had always loved and respected the firm for what it stood for. I had been the beneficiary of a lot of the programs that the firm implemented. So when this happened, I almost thought that maybe what the firm had done in the past was more marketing than anything. It was so easy for me to turn the other way. I was ready to leave myself. But when the firm approached us and was very apologetic about the situation, I felt like you should give people a chance to redeem themselves. I actually encouraged people to at least listen to the dialogue or to have the conversation with the firm to see if there was something they could do because there were a lot of other places that really couldn't give a hoot about what their minority lawyers thought because we are the minority.

I felt like the firm cared once I saw that they went through the process of getting a diversity consultant and held meetings to get a sense of what approach the firm should follow. So, based on those efforts on the part of the firm, I changed my view.

Sharon's firm probably did not intend to offend its attorneys of color. The firm just failed to consider its attorneys when deciding to represent a new client. Although the firm had a clear sensibility as far as their Jewish attorneys were concerned, it had not communicated enough with African American and attorneys of color. As more and more African Americans joined the firm, there was definitely a need to gauge the sensibilities of this new and growing population within the firm.

Organizations often do not realize how changes in their employee and client demographics may require a few tweaks to their social traditions. For instance, some companies pride themselves on sporting events that are male dominated. However, such events, while open to everyone, still have a tendency to exclude women.

Susannah Burke,* a Caucasian lawyer who practices law in Alabama, has watched her firm hire more women attorneys but fail to welcome them into the fold. As the mother of a little boy, she is sensitive to the time management and business development issues that many of the other women in the firm face. Here, she describes how gender-related events make her and female clients feel excluded.

I think primarily it comes down to marketing for my job. A lot of times the firm will market specifically toward men. I know that they may not necessarily intend to do that, but they plan events like a PGA golf tournament. They took a bunch of clients to a PGA golf tournament in Atlanta. That's great, but that's not something I'm interested in doing. I felt like one, I was excluded, and two, that there were female clients who were excluded. The invitation was extended to everyone, but because the subject matter was geared more toward men and all the clients that attended were men, it was not something that I felt comfortable attending. I did not attend.

The firm does host events that are more general. They host cocktail parties and things. But in response to events like this, the firm came up with a women's marketing group where we try to target more female clients so we have our female attorneys participating in that. I just feel like that's the wrong way to go about it. Why does everything have to be geared toward one specific group? Why can't we have more things that are applicable to everybody? I feel like there are ways to market toward women and men. You can do that within the context of one party as opposed to limiting it to one particular group.

In the context of the large cocktail parties that we have, probably the women are going to migrate toward each other. It tends to happen. There's a way to market within that. At the same time at least you're not saying, "Oh, well you have to work with me." You could say, "There's a guy who works downstairs who does the kind of work you're interested in, client, so I would like to introduce you to him." As opposed to when we are completely segregated we limit ourselves in terms of marketing. That initial bond could come from woman to woman contact, but at least you still have the men there so that you can introduce everybody and promote the firm as a whole.

I felt frustrated. I felt like the firm was not considering everyone's feelings. They only considered the people who were planning the event, who incidentally were all men.

The women's marketing group was created in light of several events like the golf event where men were going out and the women felt excluded. So there was a woman associate, who is now a partner, who decided to start the women's marketing group. We've done events specifically geared toward women. In the fall we do a wine tasting. Only women in the community are invited. Now several of the men in the firm have gotten a little bit frustrated by that because they would like to participate in the wine tasting as well.

Having the women's group is also frustrating because it is just one more committee meeting that I have to attend and participate in.

Tom Romano* is a Caucasian law firm partner in his forties who one would not immediately think would relate to Susannah's experience. However, as a religious minority, he has encountered his fair share of insensitivity through his law firm's traditions.

I'll start with the characteristic that's not the most acute, but the one that arguably fits within a protected class—religion. I was raised Catholic. I'm a mutt in terms of my background. I may have even had some Jewish in my background, but that's kind of murky. I was raised Catholic. My father's side was predominantly Polish and my mother's side was predominantly Pennsylvania Dutch and Germanic. I stopped practicing Catholicism and considered myself an agnostic. When I worked for a predominantly Jewish firm, I felt a little uncomfortable that I was not taking time off for the Jewish holidays. Ironically, I felt uncomfortable when I was working on Rosh Hashanah and Yom Kippur. I felt left out. In the history of things, my firm was one of those firms created for Jews to feel comfortable because they were not let into the white-shoe firms. I ended up marrying a Jewish woman and we're raising our daughter Jewish, and I've even given some thought to converting, but I have not had the time.

At my current firm, which is historically Irish and Italian and heavily Catholic, I felt a little weird and uncomfortable when I took off for a Jewish holiday. I felt like I had to explain myself. No one did anything that I considered to be discriminatory. Ironically, I have been on both sides of that Jewish versus Christian feeling like you are in the outsider group. No one explicitly made any comments about my religious observances. At my current firm, I do remember when one or two of the other attorneys started to talk about wanting to go home early to prepare meals for the Jewish holidays, our internal counsel asked me for help in understanding the situation better so that they could address the situation properly, which was actually a good thing. Ignorance is part of the problem, and it's always a good thing to get more information. They recognized that they were not that used to the situation and they needed to get more used to it.

The underlying theory is that even if no one is deliberately or consciously doing anything to try to make you feel like an outsider, you can still feel like an outsider. For instance, at my firm they have Friday evening cocktail parties and they never would have done this at my former predominantly Jewish law firm. I try to go home for Shabbat to see my wife and daughter. It's our one guaranteed family night to be together. It's not a big deal if I really need to stay. I've never asked for the firm to change it at this point and don't really see a need to. Ultimately, I would have felt more comfortable if they didn't have the cocktail parties on Friday nights.

Eradicating the Barrier of Insensitivity

Offensive comments, insensitive work assignments, and hurtful behavior in the workplace are often accompanied by numerous repercussions. As indicated by the testimonials, insensitivity can even become a source of workplace stress. The Anxiety and Depression Association of America found 72 percent of people who have daily stress and anxiety say it interferes with their lives at least moderately.[41] Insensitivity not only exposes organizations to employment lawsuits and complaints, but it also diminishes worker productivity by causing stress.

Bidirectional communication between employee affinity groups and senior management is a useful tool that smart organizations use to test their policies and business decisions. Companies like Darden Restaurants and Macy's have used their affinity groups to avoid culturally offensive marketing campaigns and improve their advertising to minority communities. Affinity groups are ideal for shaping the organization's business policies. Sharon Ross's firm would have greatly benefited by proposing the reparations case to its affinity groups before deciding to represent such a divisive client. Affinity groups have evolved into employee resource groups (ERGs) and are more than just party planning committees.

Organizations should not be fooled that because their employees are toughing out racist, sexist, and homophobic jokes, they are not affected by the stress of the situation. Stress can result in burnout, low morale, drug use, and violence. I'm sure that the professionals I interviewed took great pains to exercise restraint while dealing with insensitive people at work.

Lorna Williams,* a twenty-something-year-old attorney in the telecommunications industry, feels the added stress of constantly working against her manager's notions about her age and gender.

> My supervisors will use certain words like, "'You're just a girl." I'm thinking to myself, no matter how much you build your credibility, they may still see you like that. It makes me adapt and want to prove that I'm not just a girl. So it's an extra pressure that you really don't need as a minority. There's already so much that you're dealing with, you don't want that too. I was just thinking, after all, I'm still happy with my decision to work for my current employer, but those types of things can make your day go slower because these are the extra things you have to conquer. You get tired.

Insensitivity in the workplace is even more unbearable now that on average, people work an extra month and a half per year of overtime.[42] According to a survey of 1,000 Americans conducted by Good Technology, most of us are answering work-related e-mails before we leave the house, at the dinner table, and before we go to bed.[43]

Unfortunately, it is impossible to write a book including all of the comments, jokes, e-mails, and behavior that will offend. I once heard a really good rule of thumb for determining offensive conduct: if you would not say something to your grandmother, then you probably should not say it in the workplace.

When organizations take the high road, and rid their work environments of insensitive behavior and stand up for what is right, they make employees into their biggest advocates and cheerleaders. Linda Chavez* fondly remembers a time when a senior-level colleague put a cocky client in his place when he made an insensitive remark about her.

> I worked on deals outside of the United States and I was once travel-ing with a senior associate and a partner. We went to Spain to work on a transaction. The client was a bank and the conference room we were working in was filled with men. I was the only woman; I was a second-year associate. At one point, while working on an infor-mation memorandum, one of the clients, a bank executive, made a really inappropriate remark. I can't even remember what it was, but he used my name in a way that was just clearly inappropriate. There are ways in Spanish that you can play with words. The senior associ-ate looked him in the eye—now we're in a room with fifteen people and we are all drafting—and said, "Jose, does that really amuse you? Do you think that your wife would be proud of you for saying that? I think we should get back to work and if you could please focus on work and think about the things you say, that would be helpful, and if you could treat Linda with respect that would be helpful." I felt great. I love that associate to this day. It completely embarrassed the bank executive in a room with all his colleagues. So the client was clueless while my colleague nipped the situation in the bud and dealt with him directly and publicly.
>
> The firm made it a practice not to hire only the best and brightest. It made a point to hire people who had outside interests or other careers, e.g., doctors and nurses. So the people tended to be more worldly and have other interests and weren't just third-generation lawyers. Hiring people who were diverse in background might have contributed to the open and inclusive environment I experienced.

OVERCOMING THE BARRIER OF INSENSITIVITY

Realize that people still say and do the most unbelievable things. I like to think that the insensitive comments and behavior on *The Office*—NBC's hit television sitcom—are so over the top that they only make for good entertainment, but every now and then I come across a law-suit that makes the show's scenarios seem gentle. The show follows the daily interactions of a group of idiosyncratic office employees via a documentary film crew's cameras. The office manager and lead character, Michael Scott, thinks that he is attuned to the issues of diversity in the workplace, but instead he is clueless and uses outdated stereotypes to inform his interactions with employees of color, LGBT (lesbian, gay, bisexual, or transgender) employees, and women—basically, anyone who is not like him.

There was an episode where Michael outed Oscar, a gay character, and kissed him on the lips to show his acceptance of gay people. After Oscar brought a discrimination complaint against the company, which was quickly settled, he made an astute assessment about insensitivity in the workplace. When Oscar returned from his "gaycation"—the term Michael coined to describe Oscar's time away from the office while his harassment complaint was being handled—he quickly realized that while the company may have learned its lesson, Michael did not. As Oscar drove into the company parking lot driving the Lexus sports utility vehicle he received from the harassment settlement, Michael kept referring to Oscar as his gay friend. Oscar was not just another employee; he was now the gay guy. While Oscar was bothered because Michael obviously did not get it, Oscar had second thoughts about the value of changing Michael's behavior. Instead, he thought, let Michael make his stupid comments about gay people. Eventually Michael's outrageous comments and behavior would give Oscar enough evidence to bring another claim. Oscar had his eye on a home theater.

Remember, insensitivity sometimes evolves into actionable discrimination in the workplace, and there are now remedies to curb outrageous conduct. Laws such as Title VII of the 1964 Civil Rights Act and similar state and city statutes prohibit disparate treatment based on a protected class. (Protected classes include race, color, gender, national origin, and religion.) Keep a journal of anything uncomfortable that has occurred. Your contemporaneous notes will keep your memories fresh and enable you to substantiate your story for your supervisor or human resources.

Depending on the situation, try to find a direct and tactful way to let the individuals know that you do not find their humor funny or that their conduct has offended you. The traditional advice is to "act nice" so that offenders will see the error of their ways. When someone hurts you, you don't have to play nice, you have to play smart. Have a trusted cadre of friends and advisors whom you can easily contact when insensitivity in the workplace strikes. Often, we may find something offensive yet objectively it is harmless. These advisors can help you put a situation into perspective and devise a strategy for handling it. You should have at least one advisor on your speed dial.

It also helps to have friends in high places in your organization. I had the pleasure of meeting Gilbert Casellas when we were panelists at a Federal Trade Commission Diversity forum. Gilbert has served on the Board of Directors of Prudential Financial for fifteen years, a corporation that has been recognized by numerous organizations over the years for its diversity and inclusion efforts. He has also served as a member of Toyota North America's diversity advisory board for almost six years. Toyota North America also has been recognized for its diversity and inclusion activities including Diversity Inc.'s Top 50 for a number of years in a row. For the past two years he has been a member of Comcast's Joint Diversity Council and chairs the Hispanic Advisory Council of that Joint Diversity Council, and for the past seventeen years he has served as a member of the Board of Trustees of the University of Pennsylvania and chaired the Diversity Committee for several years. Obviously, he was on my short list of people to interview for this book.

He started his law career in a traditional law firm in Philadelphia that one might call "Blue Blood." It celebrated its 100th anniversary in 2012. In 1977, he was the only minority lawyer at the firm. Once, when he had been working on a matter for this client and the communications were only by telephone, the client was speechless when he met Gilbert in person: a well-dressed attorney of color with a little Latin fro and a thick mustache. Later in his career at the firm, he became the personnel partner. He would check in to see how a partner was treating his people and informally mentor other attorneys of color. There was an African American associate in particular who, from time to time, he asked how things were going and the associate would share. On a particular occasion, Gilbert was there to help this associate resolve a misunderstanding rooted in insensitivity.

One day he came to me. He was really angry and he walked into my office, closed the door, and he told me about a situation where this partner had asked him to deliver something to another firm. This was one of the partners who wanted you to work on Saturdays and Sundays and was burning people out. He had no regard for people's personal lives. He treated everyone like crap. The associate was furious because we had messengers for that. It's not like the guy was going to wait for the document to be signed, but this partner was so paranoid that he wanted the associate to take the document to the other firm. He said, "You know I'm not a delivery boy." I said you're right. I'm glad that the associate came to speak with me because he was so angry that he was at the point that he might have punched out the partner. I told the associate to go back to his office and that I would go talk to partner and I did.

I told the partner that you may not realize this, but you have got to be sensitive to the fact that the associate's perception is that he is not the messenger. He's a fifth-year associate. We are paying him all this money and you are treating him like a messenger. Get real. You and I are partners, and if you mess up it affects my ability to pay my mortgage. So don't screw up. The partner apologized to the associate expressing that he didn't intend any slight. He was just clueless.

Having influential allies in your office who can address a situation with an offending manager on a peer level can make a world of difference. A complaint coming from an intern or a junior-level employee sounds much different, and is accordingly treated differently, than a complaint coming from a senior-level manager.

Also, keep in mind that people are capable of changing. When I shared my book with some of my colleagues, they were surprised that I wrote a book leaving room for the possibility that there are people in the in-group who care about improving diversity and advancing equality in the workplace. I really do believe that there are enough people in the majority who really care about improving workplace relationships, especially with those who are in the minority.

For example, Cassandra Phillips* told me about an instance in her career that exhibits the power of awareness and the change that is possible in all of us.

I did experience a situation where being a woman made me a bit of an outsider in terms of being accepted at a private club. I was in Paris, and I was newly appointed as the American representative for the ICC Court of Arbitration. I was meeting with the arbitration committee. It was the first time I was meeting them. I was very excited to be coming from New York and meeting with these lawyers who were arbitration experts.

I went to the designated location at the appointed hour, and when I walked into the club, the person greeting me, a man, said in French that I was not allowed or permitted to enter the club through the main steps. For a moment, my first thought was I must not understand his French so I had him repeat himself. It was clear I understood him. And then I thought, is this because I'm Black or because I'm a woman? Just as I was thinking that, an older White woman approached and he would not allow her to enter the club either through the main steps. And I felt a bit relieved that it wasn't because I was Black; it was clear it was because I was a woman.

After some negotiations and explanation, it turned out that this club did not allow women to use the main stairway to go up to the private dining rooms because there were nude portraits. I don't mean pornographic, but just paintings, and the club thought they would be offensive to women. So they did not want women to use the main stairwell. When I explained that I was expected for a business luncheon and there had to be some other solution, they took me around the back entrance of the club and up the side steps. So I entered the room through the kitchen and side entrance.

There was a moment where I debated whether I should go through the back stairs or not, but then I wanted to prove a point by coming in through the back way.

All the men in the meeting (because there weren't any women on the committee) were mortified by what happened. It never dawned on them that this would happen. After the lunch, they thanked me for attending the meeting. At the end of the lunch, the men went in solidarity down the back stairs with me and never had lunch again at that place.

I felt like it was a life lesson for all of us. I could have easily decided to not attend. But I decided, I'm here to do a job and I'm going to do the job and prove the point by showing them what I had to go through to get to the meeting. It was not something they intended. It was just something they never thought about because they never had a woman in the position before. I thought that their reaction, their apologizing, going forward with the meeting and walking down the back stairs with me, said a lot about how they wanted to rectify the mistake. I went on to stay in that position for a number of years.

CHAPTER TAKEAWAYS
- The person who ignores complaints of insensitive conduct is just as guilty as the person who makes the offending comment or gesture.
- Organizations often do not realize how changes in their employee and client demographics may require a few tweaks to their social traditions.
- Bidirectional communication between employee affinity groups and senior management is a useful tool that smart organizations use to test their policies and business decisions.
- When organizations take the high road, and rid their work environments of insensitive behavior and stand up for what is right, they make employees into their biggest advocates and cheerleaders.
- Keep a journal of anything uncomfortable that has occurred. Your contemporaneous notes will keep your memories fresh and enable you to substantiate your story for your supervisor or human resources.
- Having influential allies in your office who can address a situation with an offending manager on a peer level can make a world of difference. A complaint coming from an intern or a junior-level employee sounds much different, and is accordingly treated differently, than a complaint coming from a senior-level manager.

CHAPTER 6
THE IMPORTANCE OF QUALITY WORK ASSIGNMENTS AND PROMOTIONS

We are a society driven by rewards. From the Olympic Games to most reality television shows, people will drive themselves to the limits of physical and mental endurance for the top prize. The same concept applies to the workplace. What does the top prize look like in the workplace? In 2010, Aon Hewitt surveyed employees to determine their engagement drivers and found that in North America, for three consecutive years, career opportunities topped the list.[44] Today, it is a common practice for people to barter a higher salary for leave and time away from the office. Sometimes people choose to work for organizations that pay less money in exchange for what they define as quality of life. However, there is one constant. We want the same compensation and recognition for our work as our majority colleagues receive for their work. When we are overlooked or denied opportunities that we know we deserve, we quickly lose interest in the organization and look for other opportunities.

Whether it is investment banking, the entertainment industry, the government, a nonprofit organization, or a law firm, the same concepts about equal pay and, more broadly, equal treatment apply. As Steven Levitt wrote in *Freakonomics: A Rogue Economist Explores the Hidden Side of Everything* (Harper Collins Publishers Inc., 2005), "incentives are the cornerstone of modern life." So, what are our incentives in the workplace? Based on conversations with young professionals from all backgrounds, incentives to work harder vary. An incentive could be a promotion in title, a pay raise, a corner office, or challenging work assignments. In general, minorities in Generations X and Y want to feel as though they are making a difference in an organization and are recognized for their efforts.

PAY DISPARITIES

Despite the muggy, rainy morning, I was among the tens of women packed into the Graduate Club in New Haven to hear Lily Ledbetter. Wearing a pretty pink sweater, the fighter with a charming Southern drawl told us about the years she invested in working for Goodyear Rubber and Tire Co. She joined the company in 1979 in its Gadsen, Alabama, plant. For most of her career with Goodyear, she was an area manager and one of only a few women. When I asked her how the men treated her, she described them as being courteous, calling her Miss Lilly. As they seemed to hold her in esteem on a high tree limb, they were sawing off the branch. Although she started her career making the same salary as her male counterparts, when she retired in 1998 after twenty years of service, she was the lowest paid area manager. Once she realized this injustice, she filed a lawsuit only to learn that the statute of limitations lapsed. According to Title VII of the 1964 Civil Rights Act, she had to file her complaint with the Equal Employment Opportunity Commission (EEOC) within 180 days of receiving each paycheck—over the course of twenty years.

To ensure that no other person would be similarly time barred from bringing an unequal pay claim, she championed the Lily Ledbetter Fair Pay Act, which was the first piece of legislation signed by President Obama. Now, the statute of limitations on unequal pay claims starts upon the act of *any* discrimination.

Ralph Georges* felt like an outsider in his work group because of his gender. For him, standing up and demanding an explanation for the pay disparities proved to be a liberating experience in more ways than he expected.

By every indication, performance wise, I had done all sorts of strategic initiatives for the company. But when it came time for my bonus and my stock options, they weren't even year over year reflective of past performance, which was good but not as good as the year I had done all these strategic initiatives. The bonus was flat. Instead of being a 5 percent increase, it was a 4 percent increase. The stock options were less than the year before. I asked them to explain the logic in decreasing my compensation, my bonus, my merit increase, and stock options.

I did something I had never done before. I wrote a letter to my boss and my boss's boss and did a grid that showed the year-over-year difference in my bonus and my overall compensation and juxtaposed it against my performance—the things that I worked on where I got paid more than the most recent year where I worked on more strategic initiatives and launched products and got paid less. I was very straightforward. I wrote that, "I was uncomfortable and I didn't think the bonus was acceptable based on a year-to-year comparison. I don't know how you got to this number. Please explain." Here are the facts. Here is my work and my ratings. Tell me how we got here. And I did not leave it there. I said, not only do I need someone to give me a strong sense of how we got here, but I would strongly suggest you reconsider.

At this company you can formally put in a request for your bonus and even your ratings to be reviewed and reconsidered. So in my letter, I said I would like to understand my boss's thinking, but I also would request for her to rethink the bonus and the increase given the facts that I posed. It takes a lot to formalize your concerns and appeal the decision and call into question the process and whether or not it's fair. So that was a big deal.

A day went by and my boss told me that she felt sad that I felt as though I was treated unfairly. She agreed to take a look at my situation and look into it as soon as possible. During that time frame, coincidentally, I had been approached by a headhunter about another position. I started to think, maybe there is something better out there. Maybe this is a sign that I need to take. So I ended up negotiating a deal to leave to go to an entirely different kind of environment, an enterprising environment, for more money and just a better deal. I left a number of years on the table at the company, but I had this other opportunity that seemed compelling. There was a company that wanted to embrace me and my skills and experience and pay me more than I was making at the company I had been with for ten years.

LACK OF GROWTH OPPORTUNITIES

For Nadine Lewis* the incentive was a promotion in title and responsibilities. Nadine was in her mid-twenties when she decided that she wanted to work for the public good. She joined a government agency with a class of other young attorneys who were willing to make financial sacrifices to pursue their interests in public service. As long as there were opportunities to grow professionally, they were fulfilled. However, after a few years, Nadine realized that her career was not going anywhere. She started with an entry-level title, and after three years she still held the same entry-level title. According to her title, she was only capable of basic research and required heavy supervision. However, she had matured into the office's go-to attorney. When her supervisors wanted a case handled efficiently, they assigned her to it. There were even instances where her supervisors determined that she could handle cases better than the more senior attorneys. While Nadine was pleased that her supervisors noticed her good work, she could not get over the promotion process. When she looked around the office, she noticed that no attorney had been promoted in seven years. Although she spent late nights at the office and handled the office's most complicated work, her request for a promotion in title was denied. Her supervisors were willing to give her a nominal bonus— they could not deny that she was a stellar performer—but they were not willing to tackle the bureaucracy involved with giving her a promotion. Her supervisors could not believe that she turned down their offer to give her more money, but that was in part because they didn't take the time to understand Nadine's incentives.

> I knew that my days with this government agency were numbered once I realized the limited opportunity for growth. To hold my position, I had to become a member of a union that had a collective bargaining agreement. My supervisor claimed that she could not promote me because of all the hoops she had to jump through with the collective bargaining agreement, but I felt like she was just

playing the blame game. If she wanted to promote me she could have taken the time to initiate the promotion process. While more money would have been welcomed, I was more frightened that my skills would get dull and that I would become less marketable as time went by. My supervisors could not understand this. They often looked at my class as "those young attorneys." They didn't respect the fact that we had career aspirations. I knew that regardless of how many cases I tried, settled, and mediated, future employers would always doubt my abilities if I still held an entry-level title. I was not alone in deciding to leave. I joined the agency with five other attorneys and when I left, only two remained. When I announced that I was leaving, the two attorneys who had not left yet asked me to keep an eye out for job opportunities. Who knew that even with an advanced degree there are dead-end jobs?

A media executive confided in me about a time when he felt that his career was stalled. Although he earned an MBA in marketing from a business school ranked in the top ten, he had the hardest time jump-starting his career.

Part of my reason for leaving was based on disparities. The department had about forty people and there were three Blacks. I was the most senior Black person. We were all treated as though we were not part of the company. I had made a decision after being there for almost ten years, from a career standpoint, that I wanted to experience new things and develop a different set of experiences. I made a decision to post for another position within the company. I had received very good performance-related scores during my career, but for whatever reason I could not break through and get the jobs I posted for. I was always the second runner-up or the first runner-up.

Here's the thing that's crazy. It felt like there wasn't an opportunity to grow within my group, but my group was so insular to the main body of the company that it did not allow me to bridge over to different career opportunities. I ended up being in a situation where there was no room to grow in the organization because I was not a part of the "family." It was a double-edged sword because not only was I not able to grow within the family, but there were a lot of businesses that did not feel that that organization was suitable as a launching pad for the bridge to other careers within the company. So it became almost like it was run like a separate entity, or almost like an agency. It made it difficult to find posts for positions. I told my boss and other people that I wanted to get more mainstream and find new opportunities within the broader company. I had been there for a number of years. Within a six- to nine-month timeframe, I got no traction in any other positions. There was a real challenge that caused me to really rethink if I wanted to be there at all.

QUALITY OF WORK ASSIGNMENTS

How projects are assigned is another source of feeling ostracized by the organization. Samira Hylton* was determined to address the assignment process in her office when she brought her supervisor's attention to her workload.

I had a conversation with a partner about the quality of work that I was getting and the volume. I was not happy with the volume. I felt like it was too slow, and I spoke with the partner about it. He comforted me by saying that it was a slow period for everyone, but then he threw in a little piece of advice. He told me that I should try to get to know some of the senior associates because they were the ones that the partners know and they are who they'll work with. So, if I got to know the senior associates they would recommend me for assignments. Then he proceeded to name the associates, and it was five or six White men who were in their early thirties. (At the time, I was a junior associate in my mid-twenties.) These were guys who I felt like I had nothing in common with, and the partner said I should get to know them informally. And I just wondered how I would go about doing that if it wasn't some sort of workplace thing. If I would just drop by their office and say, "Hey, let's go have something to eat or let's hang out after work," or what. At that point I felt like that wasn't a realistic piece of advice for me.

DIVERSITY OF WORK ASSIGNMENTS

Jocelyn Ade,* a transactional attorney in New York, was not so much concerned about the volume or quality of her work assignments. Instead her issue was the diversity of her work assignments.

> My situation is unusual in the sense that I was on the same case for over four years. I needed to work on different matters. I needed to see cases from beginning to middle to end, and I just wasn't getting that. The firm tried to keep me, but I knew that I would not have been happy.
>
> I left the second firm because it made promises to me about the type of work I would receive. I told them that I had only worked on larger cases and that I wanted to work on smaller cases. I was told that I would get a lot of smaller cases. While I was getting that, I was not getting to work on cases from beginning to end. I was just brought onto cases to finish up what other people had worked on.

Quick question: in Corporate America, in which two departments do you find the most minorities? Usually, you find the most women and racial minorities in the mailroom and the cafeteria. Similar to noticing when we are people in the minority, we also notice when minorities are in the majority when it comes to work assignments. Sometimes, in corporate environments, there is a direct correlation between the desirability of a project and the percentage of women and racial minorities: the less competitive the assignment, the higher the percentage of women and racial minorities staffed to the project.

Bridgette Fox,* a Yale Law School graduate who worked in New York City as a corporate attorney, could not help but notice when select assignments were relegated to the attorneys of color in her firm.

> There was an instance where I got assigned to work on a project where 90 percent of the people assigned to it were minorities. No one wanted to get stuck working on this project that was literally around the clock for six weeks straight. This was not a corporate project; it was a litigation project. I was not even doing the work

that I was supposed to be doing. I remember there was a White male corporate associate who was in the same year as me who complained about it and was taken off the same day. All of the people pulled into the project, one after another, were Asian, Indian, and African American.

I did feel in different contexts and sometimes for different reasons that I was left out of things. I felt like I was never assigned the same level of work as nonminority associates. A couple of things that I remember, specifically, were when I spoke with a partner about the type of work I was assigned and that I was not getting assigned work. Was it something about me or my work product that wasn't good?

We were assigned in units to various partners. I was in the Mergers and Acquisition (M&A) group, so there were two partners who had a handful of associates and they were supposed to assign work to them. In the group of associates, there were two racial minorities: there was an Asian fellow and me. I remember the partner saying that he had trouble getting work for me and the other guy. He couldn't really articulate any reasons for that. In my own feeling, I just thought, well, this is a person who simply doesn't want to assign work to minority associates. The two of us didn't have problem areas with our work. I knew that there were White males in the M&A group and they were getting a lot of work, good work. It made me feel pretty bad. This was a very new experience. For ten years before I went to law school I had been an executive at a large multinational commodities trading company and I had a lot of authority in that position. In my former field, the grains industry, which is very Midwestern and White male dominated, there was at least a level of respect. I really didn't feel that when I got into this large law firm environment I would be obliterated because of the way I looked or people's assumptions about me. It was hard and that was one of the reasons why I left that firm after two years.

ADVICE FOR MANAGERS

An employee's ability to grow depends on the quality of work and the level of responsibility given. If professionals are not challenged with new and exciting work, they often become bored and eventually will not become more valuable to the organization. Quality assignments and promotions usually go hand in hand. So, how does an organization limit the potential of some people getting better assignments, not because they cannot do the work but because they are not personally favored?

Chai Feldblum is the Commissioner for the Equal Employment Opportunity Commission, and she has seen her share of legitimate and invalid claims of discrimination that arise out of the assignment process. When we spoke about the micro-inequity of quality work assignments, she explained that organizations need to start by having a foundation of good management.

> Good management means that the managers are not conflict averse. The managers and supervisors force themselves to say clearly what their expectations are for quality work product so that no one is in the dark about what they need to produce. If every manager gets the right *therapy* to know how to do that, it will in fact ensure that inclusion would work better because then issues around stereotypes, for example, that it is disability or sex or religion, are not going to occur. The hardest thing now is that people are often not told whether or not they are performing well. When people feel like they are not being given the quality work assignments, it is sometimes hard to pinpoint why. When you have managers who are conflict averse who are not willing to state clearly what their expectations are, and managers who are not willing to give direct feedback on the product, you are in this murkiness and you have no idea why suddenly you are not getting a quality work assignment. The employee is left to guess at the reasons for the withdrawal of work and sometimes that guess will include discrimination. I think it's much harder to teach managers how to articulate what they want and how to give clear feedback than to teach them the specifics of a reasonable accommodation for a disability.

The next step in building a better manager is an essential dose of honest communications, especially when articulating the essential functions of the job. Commissioner Feldblum advises,

The ability to articulate the essential functions of the positions
that are being supervised should be in the job description of every
manager. The job description should also require a demonstrated
ability and willingness to provide feedback. For the supervisor, the
essence of that job is to make sure that the people working for you
achieve their job. That is the 30,000-foot issue for that supervisor.
So how good you are as a supervisor is going to depend on how
well you ensure that the people working for you are performing
their job. That's why we are paying you to supervise as opposed
to paying you to do.

And then there is the difficult hurdle of getting managers to give honest and timely feedback. The typical evaluation process involves a
bi-yearly review where managers are able to give surface responses. As
an employment lawyer, I scratched my head whenever I read a milque-
toast evaluation that read, "So and so was/is nice to work with," or "So
and so needs to improve the 'how' of their work." Whenever someone
was terminated for poor performance, the first document I wanted to
read was the performance evaluation. The best managers were brutally
honest about an employee's performance. Once, I read a manager's review
that was so thorough, specific, and detailed in describing an employee's
shortcomings that it was a wonder the employee did not voluntarily find
another job. Then, there were managers who would only communicate
feedback during those bi-yearly performance reviews, not providing any
insight or guidance during the other ten months of the year. In general,
people don't like to give feedback. It might be their personality type.
Or, they feel like they're being rude. It might be cultural. Commissioner Feldblum and I agree that you should not put yourself forward
to be a manager if you are not able to give honest, clear feedback. We
believe that in the job description for manager it should say this is a
critical qualification standard for the job. An essential function of the
job is to make sure that the people that you supervise are performing
well. That is your essential function. The classification standard is that
you are able to provide clear feedback even when it's being critical of
someone's performance.

Commissioner Feldblum explained,

> Someone should not apply for the job of a manager if they don't feel
> they can do that. If for some reason they feel like they can't do it for
> personality or cultural reasons, then they need to do some work on
> themselves before they can get that job. So often what happens now
> is that someone is a good investigator, so they say that we will pro-
> mote you to be a supervisor. But being a supervisor is very different
> than doing the job itself. It's not easy. I wasn't kidding when I said
> therapy. Sometimes people have done individual or group therapy
> and have learned tools of how to be honest so they just might be
> better managers. There are all these programs that teach you how
> to be honest. I just picked this up at this last event I was at, how to
> have difficult conversations. There is this whole enterprise, but that's
> what they do. Managers should have to go to the ten-step program
> on how to give honest feedback.

Adding the overlay of demographic difference only complicates the
uneasiness managers experience with giving negative feedback. Men have
admitted to me that they will not give harsh or critical feedback to a
woman out of fear of getting sued for gender harassment. Managers have
confided in me that they would never give a person from a historically
underrepresented background—race, disability, religion—a true evaluation if their performance was lacking because they feared a discrimination
charge and a subsequent negative public image. I could not agree more
with Commissioner Feldblum when she told me,

> Employers should not be afraid to give minorities feedback. That is,
> if the employer has set it up with that initial framework where the
> expectations for quality work are clearly articulated. Every person—
> man, woman, Black, White, disabled, not disabled—every person gets
> candid, honest feedback. If you are doing this across the board and
> you can show that one hour before you gave this kind of feedback to
> a woman you gave this kind of feedback to a guy, then you are fine.
> But it has to be understood that honest, candid feedback is given to

everyone, and if you really do that, sure, women might feel that it is gender harassment and a guy might feel it's gender harassment if a woman gives critical feedback. Anyone can feel any of those things, but the point is to have a framework for your workforce where you can clearly show that this is how we get feedback. You should not be afraid if you set up your workforce in the first place where that is just the norm. It's all about what is the norm.

THE COMFORT FACTOR

When I was launching my consulting career, I convened a panel discussion at a New York bar association that I thought was going to start a fight. The panel was a balanced mix of men, women, attorneys of color and attorneys not of color, in-house counsel, government attorneys, plaintiff's counsel, and a large corporate law firm. To stir up conversation, I had actors role-play the most common issues I saw in practicing law. One scenario featured an African American male attorney who walked past the partner and the other members of his team meeting with the client. No one had invited him to the meeting, and when he asked why, the partner responded, "Oh, I guess we forgot to include you." After the role-play, the panelists all chimed in with their interpretations of what occurred. As I wrote in chapter 1, usually it is difficult to unearth the depths of honesty that are necessary for effecting change. However, one panelist was brave enough to tell the truth: maybe the partner did not want to work with the associate because he personally disliked him. The panelist was a partner for a prominent law firm, and he admitted that he would avoid working with an employee if he didn't have anything in common with the employee. He wouldn't invite the associate to strategy meetings or include the associate in any assignments that involved heavy interaction. The room was in awe. Here was a partner unequivocally stating that his comfort with the associate could carry more weight with the assignment process than the quality of the associate's work. One of the program attendees, a former law firm associate, could not resist explaining to the partner that his attitude could be detrimental to associates whom he deemed different from him. When he continued to insist that in the assignment process, personality and familiarity would trump skill, the audience member switched her appeal-to-reason approach to proverbially dousing him with a bucket of cold water. The room shivered when she told him, "That was mighty White of you."

If supervisors have a preference for working only with people who look, act, and sound like them, they are unfairly denying all of their other employees an equal opportunity to advance within the organization and are undercutting the organization's diversity efforts. Andres Tapia, Senior Partner at Korn/Ferry International, has also found that the comfort factor plays a significant role in the assignment process.

> Every quality assignment, every promotion, every hire is always a risk in terms of who you put on it. There are no guarantees. Proof of past performance is not indicative of future performance. So you are always taking a risk. What helps managers take the risk more easily than in other situations is comfort. What leads to comfort? Unfortunately, a lot of comfort is someone like me. It's not necessarily a prejudicial thing as a classical way of prejudice. It's not necessarily an evil thing; it's actually very appealing.
>
> We know best what we know most. If we know it and the more intimate we are, the more likely we are to make a managed risk decision. I know it's a risk, but because I know this person or know people like him or her, my risk is not as great as opposed to when I hire or give someone a quality assignment who I don't know or comes from a community that I don't understand and I don't know how to mitigate my risk. So the issue of comfort is very human and very natural.

Underlying the comfort factor is the fear of vulnerability. When we make ourselves vulnerable as managers seeking to move beyond our comfort zone, we leave ourselves open to potential criticism, harsh judgment, or being wholly discounted because of the risk we will take on a person. How do you mitigate the risk?

One strategy is taking a brave interest in those who seem unfamiliar to you and increasing your exposure to groups to which you do not belong. The Stanford University study, *Why Most People Disapprove of Me:*

Experience Sampling in Impression Formation, determined that our impressions of others are biased based on positive or negative interactions and with increased interactions, there is the greater possibility of curing any false initial impressions.[45] When there are more opportunities to get to know someone, we can break down crippling stereotypes and increase our understanding and acceptance. This is why we have less fear of groups when we have a few (not the token one) from those groups. Many allies of the LGBT community explain that their support of a community once foreign to them became familiar when a friend or family member came out. People with disabilities seem more like people with diverse abilities through continued interactions.

Building upon this strategy of mitigating the risk when moving beyond your comfort zone as a manager is creating a system of strength in numbers. Andres shared the following mechanism that is working for the Federal Reserve Bank of Chicago.

> They now have hiring and promotions teams as a proxy for quality assignments by committee. So before it used to be someone tapping somebody on the shoulder saying, "Hey, I want you to apply to this job or I want you for this job." So you can imagine all of the comfort issues and subjectivity issues related to that. So, systematically a way of mitigating that is that those roles get posted and when they get posted they also post the recommendations on the part of individuals in the organization who could be candidates, so you're not just going to the hiring manager with a suggestion. You're going to the community of diverse managers and leaders to see who they would nominate or surface as a potential candidate. They do a committee-based hiring so that the candidate who they are hiring gets interviewed by a group of people, not necessarily just the hiring manager or the direct reports to the hiring manager, but even people outside of the group. That becomes a systematic way to have a check and balance against my tendency to go for comfort.

This strategy increases the chances of looking at the qualities of the candidate rather than just relying upon subjective perception. According to Andres, this system has only been in place for a few months and has already led to several very high-quality promoted people from various backgrounds. With almost every hire, the hiring manager said, "I would not have even known that this person was even in the system." The new hires were not in their circle of comfort, and this process now involves a group of people who can help the hiring managers assess candidates more fairly and not have the comfort factor overweigh other decision-making factors.

OVERCOMING THE BARRIER OF QUALITY WORK ASSIGNMENTS

Professionals in the minority should also have a strategic plan for growth. Find a trusted advisor, and have him or her help you to map milestones for your career. This will help you know if you are getting the quality and quantity of work to achieve your end goals. If you're not reaching your milestones, you will know sooner rather than later if your organization is doing enough to develop your skills. If it is not, then you can take proactive steps to improve the situation.

If you feel as though your primary work responsibilities are not giving you the challenges you want, be creative in finding other ways to enhance your skills. Volunteer projects for community and professional trade associations are a good way to build your management skills. For lawyers, pro bono projects are a good way to get exposure to a practice area and may even offer the opportunity to develop your leadership and management skills. Plus, since most organizations are grateful for your assistance, they will give you the training and guidance that you may not get in your work environment. Although it might be unpaid work, it is still resume-building work.

In 2005, the *New York Times* did a piece about how 41 percent of minority women gained leadership skills through volunteer work with their church or community organization, yet this leadership never translated into the workplace. Depending on your relationship with your manager, you may want to consider inviting him or her to an event that you have organized so that you can show off your management skills. An approach may involve *casually* telling your manager about the event or accomplishment. If you were recognized by your church or a civic organization, you should think about putting the award in your office. Awards spark curiosity, and your manager will most likely inquire about your award. If you really feel as though your manager would not care to know about your involvements outside of work that demonstrate valuable workplace leadership skills, you should strongly consider whether you are working in an environment that is right for you.

Apart from developing leadership skills, volunteer work gives you the freedom to try new things. You can work in a substantive area completely different from what your position offers. For instance, I always had an interest in learning about negotiating sponsorships with corporations because I wanted to increase my fund-raising skills. As a practicing attorney, I never had the opportunity in my day-to-day work to draft sponsorship forms. However, while serving on the National Association for Multi-Ethnicity in Communication's Programming Board, I was constantly trying to find new ways to generate funding for programs. I learned how to create sponsorship letters, media kits, and other public relations tools to get funding. Today, I use these skills on a daily basis operating my nonprofit organization.

Ultimately, the most effective strategy for advancing within an organization is to consistently churn out quality work, obviously. Bernice Washington, a brilliant keynote presenter who spent years in pharmaceutical sales, told me,

> Ironically, from my perspective I prefer to be given the most challenging task available. It has always been my goal to demonstrate that I have the capacity to do exceptional work no matter what the task may be. These may be the projects that require a lot of time and energy and seem nearly impossible to conquer. In these situations, the advantage is that there are low performance expectations because no one has been able to accomplish successful outcomes in the past. The big advantage is that if you do well, then you shine above most other people. The operative word is that you still have to *shine*. Once you demonstrate your capacity to succeed, then you are in a stronger position to ask for other opportunities.

People are more willing to listen to you AFTER you are successful. Most people want to start off in the management or CEO seat with all the glamour and the options. But there are very few people who are willing to start at the ground level and work their way up. Just the process of climbing the ladder teaches some lessons that few textbooks have the capacity to teach.

I grew up chopping and picking cotton in rural Louisiana in the smoldering heat. I knew that if I could do that job, do it well, and do it with pride, then I could do anything else that I set my heart and mind to doing. And that has always been my mind-set because the very worst thing that could happen to me is that I would have to start again from where I started before . . . *chopping and picking cotton.* When you understand and accept the maximum price you have to pay for something, it empowers you to take the risk.

Staying ahead of management has been a foolproof strategy for overcoming being overlooked. A mid-career attorney shared with me that

Clients have a tendency to *forum shop*[46] to avoid working with me. I am the only female person of color in my group. I've actually indicated to my management that I can only be useful if they copy me on responses or tell clients that I will be the one responding because I am the point of contact. So I've taken that direct approach. To certain degrees this has worked. But I still think that it's human nature for my supervisors to think, "I'll just handle it." And nine times out of ten that's not accurate because they don't know all the details of the matter. If you are one step or two steps ahead of management, they're not going to know everything. You should know information like the back of your hand. You want to make yourself more indispensable than most.

PROGRESSIVE FEEDBACK

If your work assignments are met with superficial or no feedback, there are ways to grab a manager's attention. Commissioner Feldblum shares the following strategy:

If the person is getting no feedback, send an e-mail to his or her manager saying, "Can we sit down for fifteen minutes? I just want you to tell me how you think that I'm doing." And then when you're sitting down with the person you can say, "Look, I asked for this because I want an honest and candid assessment of how I am doing because if I am doing well I'll keep doing that, and if I can do better I want to hear that."

If you're getting perfunctory feedback, for example, all this is really good but you're not feeling like you're actually getting assignments that you should be getting if you have been doing really well, then you should send an e-mail that says, "Can I get a half hour of your time?" The first meeting would be fifteen minutes because it is literally a moment to force the supervisor to stop and think about you and tell you about yourself.

But, if you're at least getting the perfunctory feedback but you're not sure that it is honest, ask for a half hour of your manager's time and explain that you would like to go over one assignment that you've done. You force the supervisor to go through it with you after he or she said it was fine. Ask whether something could have been done better. You are then giving the person an opening to dig in. Who knows, you might get some of the feedback that you have not been getting. That half hour is not to tell you how you are doing generally, because then you'll just end up in generalities again. Pick one project and force that supervisor to spend a half hour with you telling you what was good and not good.

Sometimes another way in which you may feel undervalued is being underpaid. If you suspect that you are being underpaid, you should research the issue before you take any action. There are a number of websites like Salary.com where you can compile salary information about your industry, cross-referenced with information about your level of experience. After this information is gathered, the last thing you want to do, though, is complain about not making as much money as the person sitting in the office next to yours. Your plan now needs to turn into a negotiation strategy. Ron Shapiro, author of *The Power of Nice* and agent to Major League

Baseball players and famous personalities, told me about his simple, but comprehensive approach to negotiations: Prepare, Probe, and Propose. Ask questions about your salary and listen to your boss's reasons for his salary determination. Once you have prepared and probed, think about proposals that will meet your and the organization's needs. Feel free to offer creative, but reasonable, solutions to resolve the salary gap. Aside from asking for the obvious—more money—consider proposing solutions that will enhance your quality of life: additional leave, promotion in title, flextime that allows you to arrive and leave at times that work best for you and the company, bonus, and other similar benefits.

You may also consider working with a headhunter or professional placement recruiter. Since companies are constantly contacting temporary placement agencies to fill positions, these professional recruiters know the employment market. A headhunter can assist you with your job hunt, polish your resume, and tell you how much your position is worth in the open market. To find a reputable headhunter, ask your colleagues and trusted advisors for a referral. It is always best to work with someone whose work is familiar to someone you trust.

To avoid becoming extinct to your organization, you should look for opportunities to sharpen your skills. This may involve taking courses, reading articles, and even writing articles about your area of business. Public Enemy's Chuck D, one of the most politically conscious rappers from the 1980s and 1990s, summarized the importance to staying ahead of the curve:

One Show Pony: Diversifying Your Skills Set

Young minority professionals should come into the situation where they're told that they can add diversity, then they have to look inside themselves and be diverse inside themselves. I mean that you can't come in there (and this is an unwritten rule for minorities) less equipped and with less drive than everybody else. You can't come in being a one-trick pony, being a master of just one trade. Immediately your entire department or your particular niche could be wiped away with just the stroke of a pen. So it pays to be very well schooled in all aspects of whatever business that you're trying to get into, especially when you're going into a corporation. The more things that you happen to be privy to, the more positions that you may be able to fill. There are times when your aim for a particular position happens to not be there because it's a game of numbers, a game of racism, or just the good old-fashioned game of saying that you're underqualified.

CHAPTER TAKEAWAYS

- Having a solid and consistent framework for how feedback is given in an organization reduces the validity of an employee complaining about harassment or discrimination.
- The comfort factor is a significant barrier to inclusion in the assignment process.
- Committee-based hiring takes some of the risk out of hiring someone unfamiliar to you.
- When seeking feedback, ask for a fifteen-minute meeting to get your manager to think about your work; use the thirty-minute meeting to get specific feedback on a particular project.

CHAPTER 7
DUAL IDENTITY

Jasjit Jaggi immigrated to Queens, New York, from India as a teenager. While thousands of miles away from his homeland, he didn't feel like a foreigner in Queens, a city in which over 100 languages are spoken. Many of his neighbors shared his values, attended the same houses of worship, and went to school with him. They staved off homesickness while helping him acclimate to his new home. Like most other teenagers, Jasjit had the typical after-school job at a fast-food restaurant. Although he was a good student, he could not afford college and instead spent a few years zipping through New York City as a yellow taxi cabbie. As most immigrants do, Jasjit came to America to succeed and he dreamed of doing something that would make his parents and community proud. He wanted to join the New York City Police Department (NYPD) as a Traffic Enforcement Agent.

For a few months, he spent his days studying for the NYPD entrance exam and passed it with flying colors. A few weeks later, he graduated from the NYPD's training academy as the valedictorian. He was so shy and quiet that he almost regretted being the valedictorian, which meant giving a speech to his class and their friends and family. Surrounded by his wife and two small children, he felt proud and as though he was living the American dream. When he arrived for his first day of work, he was excited to receive his work uniform. As it was given to him, he encountered his first emotional and spiritual conflict in the United States. He is a practicing Sikh and the NYPD uniform policy, at the time, was not willing to accommodate his turban. After extensive litigation, I was able to help Jasjit and the NYPD make a few changes.

How much of ourselves we display in the workplace is a serious consideration for outsiders, especially when the characteristic that puts us in the out-group is visible. Duality involves having to negotiate how much of your culture, heritage, and personality you allow to seep into

113

the office. For good reason, people in the minority are conscious of how they may be perceived in the workplace, especially if we are the only person with a particular characteristic. We are concerned about being stigmatized and stereotyped. Most outsiders understand that some level of assimilation is required to survive in the workplace. Sometimes duality involves being two drastically different people: one person at work and another at home. For instance, I had a biracial colleague who literally had two different personas, and he playfully had different names for each. He was the policy director for an organization that worked to help formerly incarcerated men re-enter mainstream society, and he worked with liberal White women who often expressed misguided generalizations about Black men and the reasons for their high unemployment rates, high incarceration rates, and other societal plights. His office persona was a suave professional who wore a suit to work every day, even though his office colleagues wore jeans and sneakers to work. When he left the office, he wore a T-shirt featuring his favorite rap artist and a leather jacket with sleeves short enough to reveal the tattoos running up and down his arms. Although he felt more comfortable in casual clothes and was proud of his tattoos, which held personal significance and told his life story, he feared that his colleagues would see him as a thugged-out Black man and clutch their purses as he walked by. He was concerned that his credibility as the office expert would be questioned and it would be more difficult to get his job done. So to keep things simple, he dressed the part to play the part.

The concept of "bringing your whole self to work" is a platitude that even the experts shun. Andres Tapia, president of Diversity Best Practices, explained to me that "bringing your whole self to work" is "beautiful rhetoric that is not realistic." He went on to say,

> If you believe that *bringing your whole self to work* is truly going to happen as a minority, you are deluding yourself for a few reasons. One, I have rarely seen an organization live up to that. Two, even if you have an organization that's really willing to do a lot of that, in the end there is such a thing as organizational culture. It's a reality. It's not like you can impose who you are on a blank slate. Organizations are like people—many have a certain way of doing things. And, you have to know where it is that you are going to stretch and adapt to them and where you're going to help them flex and adapt to you. Organizations understand that they have to stretch in a reciprocal way and adapt to the employees that are diverse that are coming in. It is a dance.

Kellye Whitney, editor of Chicago-based *Diversity Executive* magazine, and I also had an opportunity to discuss the "whole-self" propaganda that never seemed to make its way from the diversity training room to our desks.

> At the end of the day we don't necessarily really want people to bring their full self to work. It's one of those lip service-y type statements that people who have great intentions make, but what they are really trying to do is open the environment and make it welcoming to new ideas and to difference; that's admirable. That is something that should be promoted and celebrated. Without the proper context, however, bringing your whole self to work is kind of silly because no one—whether you are a minority or a man—really wants that. Some facets of me are not appropriate for the office, nor are they necessarily relevant to the work that I do or how I contribute to my organization's mission. That's why companies have rules. What they want is for you to feel comfortable enough to share what's on your mind, and that's necessary because information and diverse

perspectives are important if you're going to be successful in today's global marketplace. The breadth and scope of products and services that companies have to offer, to a varied group of customers, clients, patients, and employees, by necessity has to be vast, yet targeted. That means diversity is a requirement to compete on a global scale. Comfort is great—it facilitates engagement, retention, it can enable knowledge sharing, the talent management benefits are many, but organizational culture and business relevancy are just as important.

Outsiders can feel misunderstood and "othered" when an aspect of who they are is dramatically different from the in-group and it requires work to fit in with the majority culture. A 2006 article in *Essence* magazine, "How Black Can You Be? African Americans on the Job," explored this issue of dual consciousness. Ronald Brown, PhD, president of Banks Brown, a management consulting firm in San Francisco, told *Essence* magazine, "For Black women, one of the issues around corporate image has to do with the difference in hairstyles. For instance, when a woman wears dreadlocks in a corporate environment, the core message others receive is that you are probably more involved with your own culture than the corporate culture. There may be the sense that you're rejecting the very culture that's made the rest of us successful." *Essence* magazine reinforced Dr. Brown's observations with an interview with a Black woman television anchor who covered her twists with a straight relaxed wig when she was on the air. In the article she summed the issue up with one question, "As long as [Caucasians] have a problem with your just being here, why should you give them something else to have a problem with?"

In 2007, a *Glamour* magazine editor took the speculation out of the perception of Black women's hair. As an invited guest at a Cleary Gottlieb summer women's event, this editor called afros "political and a no-no" and dreadlocks "dreadful" during a slide presentation about corporate style.[47] People in attendance described the mood as uncomfortable and tense when the lights were turned on, revealing the women attorneys in attendance who wore dreadlocks and low-cut afros. Follow-up panel discussions were hosted by various organizations in the beauty industry to address this misstep. Image activist Michaela Angela Davis was a speaker on one of those panels. Known for her trademark blonde afro, Michaela turned to a fellow panelist and asked, "What do you see when you see me and my hair?" Michaela described the editor as turning beet red and stammering. It was probably the first time that the editor had to articulate her thoughts about a natural aspect of African American women that makes us outsiders—our hair.

While most of us recognize the importance of exercising discretion with how much we reveal about ourselves to our managers and coworkers, it is important to analyze how the decision to leave portions of who we are out of the workplace affects how we negotiate relationships at work. While some people in the minority just accept as a fact of life that they are not going to express their personality through their style of dress, hairstyles, or any other cultural indicator, others really struggle with limiting manifestations of who they are in the workplace.

Katrina Donaldson* felt as though she had to slip into a cultural straitjacket when she spent a summer in Mississippi working for a law firm. For six weeks that summer, she hid her personality, culture, and other minority characteristics.

It was not until I worked as a summer law clerk for an all-White law firm in Mississippi that I understood W.E.B. DuBois's concept of dual consciousness. When I first studied W.E.B. DuBois and his metaphor of "the veil" to describe Black Americans' dual identities in a majority White society, I was a college sophomore taking my first formal African American history class. At the time, I had no context for understanding DuBois's simple principle. All my life, I had lived and learned in environments where I felt completely comfortable to be me. Most of the students in my high school were Caribbean-American, and the teachers, White and Black, had the sensibilities for nurturing us. Even college, where I was sometimes the only Black student in a class with fifty students, was an accepting environment to people of color. For instance, my study partner for my African American history class was a White Jewish girl from Oklahoma, and she clung to urban culture much more than I did. She was very much aware of—and sometime more sensitive than I to—racial disparities and inequalities in society. This was the norm for most White students on NYU's early 1990s liberal campus. I didn't realize how spoiled I was.

I was used to working in environments where almost any look was acceptable. In one year, I went from sporting a Halle Berry bob to heavy fat braids that reached down the middle of my back. I did not feel inhibited in any way. I was very comfortable when I walked through the doors of the office, whether I was coming or going.

I got a quick wake-up call that being Black meant being different during an interview for my first job with a law firm in Mississippi. Two junior White male associates took me out for coffee after my first set of morning interviews. I thought everything was going well. After a few minutes of small talk, the associates broke down and explained that I would be the firm's first Black associate. Now this was not a new firm. They had been in existence since the 1800s. I couldn't believe that in 1999, I was going to become their first Black associate. But even more shocking was the conversation. As the associates tried to explain their commitment to increasing diversity within the firm, I no longer felt like a qualified candidate. Instead, I felt like the Black candidate. I no longer felt like one of them. I felt a division between my world and theirs. I knew that my experiences in the firm would be different than theirs. I knew that I would be seen differently and that the firm—from the partners to the support staff—would treat me as someone different. When I returned to the office for the afternoon interviews, I paid close attention to those partners, associates, and support staff I met in the halls. I was conscious of how my conduct might shape these people's perception of a Black associate.

During that summer, I left much of my personality at home to keep things simple. It was hard enough convincing these old gray-haired Southern men that I was qualified to work for the firm; I didn't need any additional hurdles. I wore my hair in a bun, I dressed in safe—and drab—corporate attire and never spoke about cultural or racial issues. The last thing I wanted was for any aspect of my

Caribbean identity to become office fodder. The veil had finally descended and it separated me from the firm.

Kenneth Wong,* an investment banker, looked around his office upon arrival and noticed that there were very few people in management who looked like him. This observation changed the way he saw himself advancing within the financial center. "Not seeing any or very few managers who were people of color on my floor made me feel excluded. I mean, I saw mostly Caucasian males and a couple of Caucasian females as managing directors, vice presidents, or above on my floor and probably in the company while working at this investment bank. I felt like there was a glass ceiling; that there would have to be a lot of conforming; a lot of, possibly, dilution of cultural identity in order to ascend through those ranks."

Without saying a word, sometimes the duality is forced upon us when others point out our differences through their assumptions of who we are. Rodney Barkley* is the typical easygoing northern California type who tries to only see one race, the human race. However, within his work environment, the cable industry, he is often nominated as the race expert on all things African American because he is African American. Occasionally, Rodney has to distinguish for his colleagues the difference between his opinions and those of African Americans. He has to explain that African Americans are not a monolithic group and each person in the race has unique and individual experiences that shape their world outlook, opinions, and aspirations—similar to how his majority colleagues demand to be seen as individuals.

I've been very fortunate to work with some very good people that have never made me feel uncomfortable or feel that I was different because of my minority status. Actually, it's kind of worked in reverse. There have been instances where I have been asked questions as if I am an ambassador, if you will, when discussing the subject of race. I look at that as, well, people are naturally inquisitive and they have questions that they would like to ask and I'll be more than happy to answer. I would always preface my responses with, "Well, I'm no ambassador for the entire African American group. I think you'll have to go talk to them individually. But, I can share with you some of my experiences based on perceptions and issues that seem to have a different slant if you are a person of color versus being a Caucasian person." But I've never, at least to my knowledge, been made to feel uncomfortable based on being a minority.

There's two ways of looking at being involuntarily placed in the position of spokesperson. You could look at it and say, "You're pointing me out because I am someone who is different." But, I also think that there is an equally balanced opposite reaction. People are really interested in what I have to say as an individual. Because of my unique perspective, being a person of minority status, I provide insight into perceptions that could possibly get the person asking the question to think about what it is that they're thinking in terms of how they perceive people who are not like them. And that's how I always took that line of questioning. I never took it as a negative.

Melody Barnes, former senior White House advisor to President Obama, learned when she was a law firm associate that perceptions about your identity come from multiple directions and shape your work environment.

Everyone has an instant impression of who you are professionally—and they act on it. I remember walking down to the firm's copy center and almost everyone there was a person of color. When I walked in, I was greeted with, "Hey, what does your boss need done?" A few minutes later, they realized that I was a lawyer—not the administrative assistant. I was the same person, but how I was perceived suddenly shifted and how I was treated shifted dramatically. Folks got more formal and stiff—and I tried to mitigate that—but there was also a clear sense of pride, which was thoughtful and also spoke to how few people of color were lawyers in big firms. Then, ten floors up one evening, I was standing in front of a partner's office looking for him, when another partner walked up and said to me, "Where's your boss?" meaning and assuming that I was the administrative assistant.

Big law firms are inherently competitive and stressful environments. But in addition to the normal pressures, I also realized that I had to navigate and manage the professional assumptions that were being made about me. Some were innocuous, but I realized that others were being made by those whose conscious or subconscious impressions would shape the future. It meant I was thoughtful about the way I treated those doing work for me and conscious about how I was being received by people who were making decisions about the quality of my work and the kind of work I was getting. I think that's a challenging situation for people of color to walk into, particularly because there were so few when I was there and there are still so few who are there now.

Eradicating the Micro-inequity of Dual Identity

One of the worst experiences one can have in the workplace is to share something personal—your culture, your life experiences, etc.—and to have someone mock you or think that you are not human, that you are an alien. With good reason people in the minority are careful as to what they reveal about themselves in the workplace.

Identity is more than just self-expression. It is about determining how much of oneself to invest in an organization. If the organization seems to embrace people who look like you, chances are that you will stay and grow with that organization because there is, or at least appears to be, an opportunity to advance. No one wants his or her identity, the parts that are important to us, stifled. The pictures on our desk, the trophies on our walls, and the art we display are all aspects of who we are. However, if it appears that anything outside of the mainstream is not accepted, then the grin-and-bear-it approach kicks in. The survival mechanism is triggered. How long do you stay in an organization that does not allow you to be who you are?

During recruiting events and interviews, create opportunities that will give prospective candidates a beyond-the-brochure look at your organization's culture. Take potential candidates on a short walk through a department so they can get a true visual of your organization—a visual that goes beyond any brochure or website. Also, design a formal process that gives candidates opportunities to learn more about your organization from people who share a similar background (e.g., school, home state) that is meaningful to them. You never want to assume that a candidate wants to speak to a "fellow" minority in your organization because when you do, you risk making the person feel "othered." The Asian candidate does not necessarily want to speak to an Asian employee to learn more about an organization. There are other aspects of the minority candidate's personality that might be more meaningful to understanding whether he or she will feel comfortable in a given work environment. For instance, the candidate may be more interested in knowing your organization's office culture as it relates to gender and family. The candidate may even want to get a sense of the extent to which people in your department socialize at work and outside of the office. Offer a range of areas about your firm that candidates can learn more about. Leave it up to the candidate to determine which qualities and characteristics about your firm are most important for them to pursue. The following interviewee offers a good strategy for creating more openness in recruiting:

360-Degree Interviewing: Giving You and Me an Opportunity to See If There Is a Fit

For the most part I'm a strong-willed person and I always felt like I didn't have to conform. Part of the reason why I went to my first firm was that I felt like I was given the freedom of expression and that I didn't have to adhere to any particular beliefs or whatever the firm image was. For the five and a half years I was at the first firm, I wore my hair braided, twisted, or in some kind of natural hair style. In fact the firm liked my hairstyle so much that I was featured in their brochure. I was in the firm's brochure for the longest time. The firm cared more about the quality of your work as opposed to what you looked like, as long as the client was pleased with your performance.

That's one part of the reason why I went to the firm. When I did my interviews, I wanted to go to a place where I could wear braids, where I could wear my glasses, slacks, and so on. During my interviews, those were some of the questions I asked. I wanted to know whether I was free to express myself or if I had to sit in a closet and be quiet. I declined offers from places where I was told, "This is not the type of place where you can express yourself. Your opinion does not count." In fact, I recruited heavily for the firm for several years. They consulted me on a lot of issues. They implemented a lot of my ideas. For instance, I had suggested that when minority students interview with the firm, the firm should ask which individuals they want to meet. Do they want to meet with individuals from the same school, individuals from the same ethnic background, the same cultural background, and so on, to make the student candidates feel comfortable asking those questions. That became part of the protocol at the firm. Our recruiting department was all White. There wasn't a Black person there. One of the things I told them was if you're a person of color, you're not going to feel comfortable saying, "I want to speak to someone who's Black." But, if you presented the option to the candidate that they could request to speak to somebody of their own color, for instance, "Is this something that you're interested in?" then the students are more likely to say, "Sure. Why not?" So that was one of my ideas. I know that I was consulted regarding recruiting issues, especially when it came to bringing more minorities to the firm. But I do feel like the firm could have done more with respect to retention. In that area they were lacking. They did better and better with recruitment, but then that fell off too. Every firm has its flaws, I guess.

When I interviewed with the firm, I met with over seven attorneys and then I came back again and then I met with three minority associates. You go through the spiel where you ask about the firm's culture and all of that. And they give you an opportunity to ask real questions. I asked the question about wearing braids. It turns out I met with an associate who had dreadlocks and I met with another associate whose hair was natural.

When I interviewed at another firm, which shall remain nameless, I phrased my question in such a way that the associate told me not to come to the firm. They didn't treat their minorities very well. The only reason she would suggest that I work for that firm was to practice in a particular practice area, which I won't name. Based on that, I declined the offer.

At my second firm, it was all about the politics. You weren't allowed to be yourself. You had to be a token Black person. You were there for color purposes only. You really couldn't express an opinion, especially one that was different from the norm. You couldn't dissent. You couldn't disagree with anything they had to say. It was a no-no. Even the people who were in the in-crowd could not disagree. The culture of the firm was so different. It's hard for me to curb my mouth. I've always felt that if you don't want to hear the answer from me, don't ask the question. In my second firm, they always asked the question. But for the most part, since no one disagreed then whatever the firm's position was went uncontested. When I came around, things were different. I was the only Black person in the entire department. I was one of four Black people in the NY office. The firm had more than 200 attorneys. They had a serious problem with attrition because of their policies.

I now have my own law firm and I feel fulfilled by it because I get to call the shots. All of the organization skills I developed at my first firm have helped me tremendously in managing my business.

As for asking questions, genuine interest in learning more about the next person with the aspiration of understanding is always a good idea. However, take a moment to think about how your question will be received before you ask it.

THE LAW FIRM HOUSE OF HAIR

One time I came to work with my hair braided. A senior associate asked me in front of the secretaries and everybody, "How do you wash that?" I answered, "I braid it and wash it and then braid it back. What do you mean?" The associate was a man. I was offended and I wondered, how does this concern you? It's hair. I wash it. I'm clean. We weren't friends and we didn't talk about beauty secrets together, so he was not asking in that regard. He was sort of saying, "You're different and let me point it out." And that was my take on the situation. I don't want to be known for my cultural differences and how I want to wear my hair. I want to be thought about for good work. I don't want to be thought of as the person who is always on her own. That's the difficulty with racial discrimination. People can always find a reason to say you don't fit in because . . . , but no one is ever going to blatantly link it to race. You just conclude that you don't fit in because of cultural differences.

Before asking questions, think about whether your questions are making someone a spectacle. Is your question too intrusive for the relationship that you have? Are you asking your question in the most sensitive way possible? If you are going to ask personal questions, try not to stereotype or ask the person questions that sound as though he or she is the ambassador for an entire group of people. For instance, if you rarely speak with a person, you really don't have the right to ask about his or her hygiene as it pertains to hair or any other cultural display. To make a person feel more comfortable with answering your questions, try to provide a few answers yourself. For every question you ask, you should be prepared to provide similar information about yourself. For instance, if someone speaks with an accent and I ask where they are from, I have a duty to share that I am asking the question because the accent sounded familiar because I visited their country; both of my parents speak with accents; or I have always wanted to learn a second language. The exchange of information diffuses a situation from an interrogation into an exploratory conversation.

OVERCOMING THE MICRO-INEQUITY OF DUAL IDENTITY

Pay close attention to the environment and the people you meet during the interview. The interview is a mutual vetting opportunity for you and the employer. This is your chance to interview your potential employer to find out more about its ethos. Use the interview as a chance to vet the company and determine whether you would be comfortable working within that organizational culture.

Fitting in by toning down your dress is not necessarily a bad thing; you should not be afraid to fit in. However, you should have a plan for what you will do with the skills and power you acquire once you have gained access to the executive suite. If you stay in the organization, are you going to change the corporate culture by encouraging more cultural expression? How will you contribute to creating a culture in which employees of all different backgrounds feel included?

Christina Hernandez,* a young corporate attorney, fit in to navigate her way through her law firm.

> I felt very comfortable about my workplace. I really was. I have not experienced that discomfort. I enjoyed working with these folks who were perhaps different from me. I had the attitude that I was going to learn from them. If I needed to adapt, I would. I was not going to change who I was or anything like that. But if I needed to behave a certain way because that was the way the room behaved, that was OK with me.
>
> I am probably in the minority in this experience because at my first firm there were several other Asians, Hispanics, and African Americans. Those guys left the firm before I did, and I think some of them left because they did not like the environment because they felt uncomfortable. I just never felt that discomfort, I don't know why.
>
> I think the firm tried very hard to recruit minorities. They had an issue with retention and they recognized the issue. When I was leaving, they tried very hard to keep me because they were losing racial and ethnic minorities and people from other cultures and they could not figure out why. They were trying to create an environment where people felt comfortable.

Although we spend the most hours of our days in the workplace, it is important to understand that the workplace may not be all things to us. It is not necessarily going to give you personal fulfillment or complete you. You may not have anything in common with the people in your office. This should not frustrate you or discourage you from advancing within the organization.

Roxanne,* a television advertising sales executive for a major television network, takes the approach that as a person of color she just wants to blend in.

> For the majority of my work experience I have been the only Black person. Early in my career, I was the only Black person in the New York sales office of over 300 people of a prominent media company. You learn quickly to assimilate. You can be Black but not too Black: to further explain, more like a person who is like everyone on the team (in the office) but just happens to be Black. You don't promote your blackness, your Black culture, or socialize only with the other Blacks (which Blacks tend to do). It is easier to just do as the Romans when in Rome.

Roxanne keeps her life balanced by creating or joining groups that feed her cultural interests. Even though you might not be able to wear hairstyles or the clothes that express your personality, you can have a base of friends or join an organization that allows you to do so. Consider joining affinity-based professional trade organizations and social organizations where you can meet others who share your social and cultural interests. Such organizations offer camaraderie and the opportunity to discuss similar feelings about issues such as dual identity and how each person handles the situation. The relationships that you develop outside of the workplace may fill the void of not seeing or interacting with people who share your interests. As I mentioned in the chapter about informal mentoring, professional trade organizations not only fill a personal interest but may also provide skill-building opportunities.

CHAPTER TAKEAWAYS
- Dual identity involves having to negotiate how much of your culture, heritage, and other aspects that make you an outsider you allow to seep into the office.
- Everyone has an instant impression of who you are professionally—and they act on it.

- If you believe that *bringing your whole self to work* is truly going to happen as a minority, you are deluding yourself for a few reasons.
- During recruiting events and interviews, create opportunities that will give prospective candidates a beyond-the-brochure look at your organization's culture.
- Designing a formal process that gives candidates opportunities to learn more about your organization from people who share a similar background (e.g., school, home state) that is meaningful to them gives candidates an opportunity to feel a sense of community, which could lead to more successful hires.
- Before asking questions, think about whether your questions are making someone a spectacle or the ambassador for an entire group of people.

CHAPTER 8
ASSUMPTIONS, SLIGHTS, AND OTHER ANNOYANCES

There are things that annoy each one of us. Maybe it's the sound of the bathroom faucet dripping in the middle of the night. It could be the sound of your coworker's shoes squeaking as she walks by your desk. Even worse, it might be how your client or supervisor gives you an assignment at 4:45 P.M.—when you didn't have anything to do all day—and wants it on her desk by the first thing the next morning. Basically, it is those little things that you sometimes cannot address in the first instance but still get under your skin.

In the workplace, employees in the minority experience subtle slights and annoyances of a different flavor. We notice how we are treated differently from our majority colleagues, who may get a nicer office or a better parking space. It is noticing that in some way, your supervisor treated someone newer and less qualified, and not in your out-group, preferentially. It could also be a rude remark. It could be something so petty that you sound ridiculous mentioning that it occurred. Sometimes it is an experience that is not significant enough to complain about but it is enough to make you feel unwelcomed.

When Lupe Dominguez* worked for a financial services firm, she was initially hired as an account representative but occasionally found herself lumped in with all of the other Latina employees as a receptionist. To her bosses, whether her last name was Dominguez, Martinez, or Hernandez, it was all the same to them. Since all of the receptionists were Latina and Lupe was Latina, they concluded that Lupe could double as a receptionist. On more than one occasion, Lupe's managers tested this flawed syllogism to her dismay.

When I was working in banking, I worked in a call center, so not only did I field calls and work in financial services but I was

129

asked to train new employees. And then, when the secretaries of the group leaders were out—all the secretaries were Latina—I was asked to fill in for them. I have no secretarial skills. I have no typing skills. I have never been a secretary, yet out of the entire department they came to me because I was the only Latina staff person. In their minds, when the two Latina secretaries are out, they thought I should fill in. Literally, they came up to my desk and asked me to fill in for the secretaries, and I complained about it. I said I don't know why I'm being asked to do this. I have a degree in journalism, I'm not a secretary. I'm training half the staff and I'm answering calls, and you want me to be a secretary too? And they said, "Well, that's because you can handle the work." That was not why.

There were several instances where it was just assumed that I was bilingual because I have a Spanish surname. No one ever asked me if I was bilingual. It was just assumed and I was given documents to translate. I was put on the telephone with customers who did not speak English. I was just told to speak to them in Spanish without ever being asked if I was able to do that. And when I couldn't do it, or refused to do it even when I could have, it seemed as though I was being insubordinate when in fact I wasn't. I'm not fully bilingual; I'm not fluent in Spanish. I was raised in an English-speaking household. But, because of the way I look, because of my Spanish surname, the assumption was there and it was across the board at this predominantly White corporate environment.

I complained to the group leader in my department. At that time, I was twenty-two years old. I was told that I was being too sensitive.

Although we have all been subjected to assumptions and slights, people of color, women, and some employees with disabilities are greater targets because we are visibly different from our White male colleagues. It is easier to pick us out. Being underestimated for no other reason than a personal characteristic is annoying. It is frustrating to be denied an opportunity to advance because you are not deemed qualified as a result of what you look like instead of how you work.

Subtle slights and small actions, which annoy a person in the minority, may seem minuscule, but they accumulate. After a while, they build and may erode employee-employer relationships and eventually cause minority employees to lose their loyalty to the organization.

Kea Jamison* left a promising career as a lawyer because of the accumulation of the subtle slight of being left out of meetings.

Every Monday morning I knew what to expect when I walked into the office. The partner who gave me assignments would be in a meeting with Isaac,* the other associate, to discuss his caseload. The meetings usually lasted an hour and were held behind a closed door. Sometimes I would hear laughter seep through the doors. When the meeting was over, they would leave the conference room together as though they were old buddies. Isaac walked out of each meeting knowing what the partner expected of him for the week. Isaac knew his responsibilities and had a clear direction for the rest of the week, thanks to the assigning partner.

I was never invited to these meetings, and I resented feeling left out. "Why would I be upset when Isaac had his meetings?" you are probably asking. Didn't I have my own meetings? Although I asked for a weekly meeting similar to Isaac's, I didn't have the same quality of meetings as Isaac. For a couple of weeks, the partner carved out twenty minutes to meet with me. But then each week, the partner would ask if we could reschedule. Eventually, the meetings were permanently postponed.

Each week as I struggled to juggle a full caseload, on my own, I would have flashbacks of watching Isaac and the partner hamming it up. This partner, who rarely gave me assignments face-to-face, had an entire hour to devote to Isaac. When I spoke with Isaac about how those meetings made me feel excluded, Isaac would always say that the meetings were no big deal. The partner and Isaac were White men, while I was the lone Black woman associate. Why didn't the partner make time to meet with me? To allay my concerns, Isaac would describe the meetings as "punitive." By trivializing the meetings, he made me sound as though I had blown things out of proportion. But I didn't. Maybe the Monday case meetings, per se, were not a big deal, but combined with the absence of mentoring and support, they were unbearable to watch and experience.

After a while, those Monday meetings were like a cavity and they rotted every aspect of my work experience. Because the partner would not have case review meetings with me and was usually unavailable, I was left to figure out everything on my own. Instead of asking the partner a question where I could get an answer in five minutes, I would spend one hour researching the answers. The partner's small slight of not meeting with me at least once a week like he did with Isaac had a detrimental effect on my work and my ability to contribute to the office. I started to lose confidence in my work and in my abilities. When the US Supreme Court decided the *Burlington Northern & Santa Fe Railway v. White*[48] case in 2006, I knew that I was not crazy. Although it was a retaliation case, our nation's highest court recognized that when a boss extends an invitation to some members of his staff and not others, especially when mentoring and training are involved, he could hinder the excluded employee's professional development. Each Monday that I watched Isaac meet with the assigning partner, I was denied mentoring and training.

Felix Johansson* is an African American television anchorman in the Midwest. The subtleties in his colleagues' and supervisor's interactions with him reflect a constant struggle for respect. While his White male colleagues are given wide latitude with what they say and how they say it, Felix knows that he must be more careful to avoid any stereotypes of being the newsroom's angry Black man.

> As a Black male I have to watch myself because I'll be perceived as an angry Black man. I feel like if I get upset about something, people immediately say that I'm giving them attitude. When another person feels strongly about something, they're passionate.
>
> One day this reporter who does not come up with good stories came up with the idea of covering whether business was going well for retailers during the holiday season. Now, who couldn't come up

with that story? What a lame story. You can do that story anytime. Last week she pitched a story about how gas prices are up. The assistant news director said, "Well we've done that story. What else can we do about this story?" Later in the meeting, all of a sudden it turned into a good story for me to do. I asked why it was a good story for me to do and suggested that the person who pitched the story cover it. After the meeting, I said, again, that I did not want to do a story about gas prices because the story I pitched was better. I pitched a story about how local churches were building homes and shipping them to Louisiana. We should do a story that affects our community. The news editor told me that I did not have to cover the story. The assistant news editor, however said, "If it was up to me, you would be covering the gas prices story." I asked why. She then asked why I was giving her attitude. I spoke to her privately and reminded her that I put 100 percent into everything that I do. I told her that as a Black male I'm perceived to have an attitude if I don't agree with something in the workplace. She then accused me of playing the race card.

There is another reporter, a White male in his fifties and he's been in this market for twenty years. Sometimes, the reporters will pitch a story and he'll say, "That's a bunch of bullshit. I'm not doing this story. It's stupid." This reporter will even step out of the camera if there is a live shot at the last minute. He won't do it, and he's right. You should never do anything that makes you look bad on-air. He does this all the time. Why is it when he objects to doing a story, it's OK. It's brushed off as Joe* is just being Joe. But when I say that I don't want to do a story, I'm giving everyone attitude. The assistant news editor said, "That's because he makes his objections and moves on." I said he moves on because he doesn't do the stories he doesn't want to do. She went on to justify his behavior by saying, "He's been in this market for a long time." I explained to her that it doesn't matter. Covering stories is his job. I explained that there was a double standard.

If I was younger, I would let this eat me up. I would come home and be in a bad mood and take my anger out on people around me.

I would come to work with a bad attitude and a chip on my shoulder. I just remember to do the best that I can and to have a positive attitude. I go to a good church with a progressive ministry and I'm just reminded about how blessed I am. I read over my notes from church and remind myself to not let people steal my joy. I know better, so I'm always going to smile. I still have to say that I have a great job.

ERADICATING THE MICRO-INEQUITY OF ASSUMPTIONS, SLIGHTS, AND OTHER ANNOYANCES

Subtle slights, annoyances, and assumptions are unnecessarily dangerous to an organization because they often lead to claims of discrimination and harassment. While courts require employees to meet various tests to establish the threshold of a discrimination complaint, all it takes is an assumption, slight, or other annoyance to spark a complaint. Each year, the Equal Employment Opportunity Commission, which enforces federal antidiscrimination laws in the workplace, receives over 70,000 complaints. I am not suggesting that these complaints are not legitimate, however. As a former employment lawyer representing employees against management, I can assure you that many of those complaints were the result of subtle slights and annoyances.

For instance, I once had an African American client, we'll call him John, who distrusted his employer and did not believe that he was laid off because his position was eliminated. Instead, he believed that his boss was a racist. Why? Because, the boss, a White male, would not say "hello" to him, while he would greet all of the other employees, who happened to be White.

When a supervisor fails to extend the same treatment, especially respect and courtesy, to all employees, the slighted out-group employee may feel the sting of exclusion. Although an organization may feel that its corporate goodwill overcomes slights and annoyances, think again. Have you ever noticed that it is easier to remember the bad things that someone did to you versus the good? Professor Roy F. Baumeister, a professor of social psychology at Florida State University, co-authored a study where he found that the psychological effects of bad memories outweigh those of the good ones.[49] In fact, he and his fellow researchers found that you need five good events to outweigh the negative physiological impact of a bad event. Even our memories of negative experiences are more accurate than our memories of positive events. Your employees are more likely to remember a rude remark or the failure to say "hello" much better than they remember the company outing. Although it seems like common sense that managers should know better than to treat employees in nondominant out-groups like second-class citizens, it happens. As the twenty-first century adage about diversity in the workplace goes, "Companies get diversity; it's their managers who don't." For proof of this schism, just look at any company that is recognized for its diversity efforts. I guarantee that you will find that the same company has employees who lodged discrimination complaints.

Often, when we talk about diversity and specifically respect in the workplace, it is in abstract concepts. Managers are told to "value" their employees, "develop" their skills, and "motivate" their workforce. However, managers are rarely given a road map to figuring out how to achieve these goals with concrete steps.

Stephanie Murray's* experiences give managers a rare glimpse of what types of conduct and behavior have negative effects on their workforce.

Subtle adversity requires people of color to endure extra, unnecessary steps that the majority does not face. I've had numerous discussions with various individuals (women or people of color) who have faced various types of adversity where they felt marginalized by the "majority's" actions. Adverse actions based upon discriminatory factors prompt me to step up to the plate even more to ensure that I do not yield power to the majority or anyone who does not have my best interest in mind.

You can't and would not want to flee from being a woman, a person of color, or a youthful-looking individual. These factors are especially relevant when the people in executive or leading roles are primarily much older, White, or male. Many of the adverse situations I have faced involved situations where I had to fight for a leadership role or to work on a high-profile project. For example, a Caucasian deponent walked out of a deposition room after learning

I was not an observer in the room but the attorney who was taking the deposition. My Caucasian colleagues uneasily smirked and took no actions. A definitive answer will never exist as to whether the deponent thought, "Oh, she's 1) too young or 2) just a silly woman or 3) just that person of color, who didn't get it and is not going to waste my time." But, one can logically deduce the deponent's thoughts fell into one of the three categories since we had not previously met or spoken.

Under this and similar circumstances, I focused on what I needed to do to prove myself and how I could/can maximize upon the adverse situation. Once I reminded the deponent that he was under a subpoena to return to the room for the deposition, he did so reluctantly. I seized the opportunity. In the deposition, I asked so many different questions in so many different ways that neither the deponent nor his attorney could keep track. By the end of the deposition, the deponent started to respect me and ignore his attorney. Certain individuals might talk to or at you like you're a two-year-old or call you endearing names (e.g., girl, darling, sweetie, son, etc.) or use colloquial terms (e.g., my bad, whassup, etc.) when you are supposed to be conducting business and you do not have a personal relationship.

Employers should be mindful of their stereotypes and assumptions. Employees are people with individual personalities, likes, and dislikes. While there is research that we do a better job of distinguishing our own-race faces than others—falling into the trap that "they all look alike"—it is still annoying.[50]

Lalia Bhindra* was the only Asian attorney and one of two women of color in her law firm. After a few similar encounters of mistaken identity, she started to feel as though she was not seen as or treated as a person but instead a color. "It was bizarre how people confused me with the other associate of color. I would send an e-mail and ask for something and then all of a sudden someone would walk into her office and say, "Hey, you know that e-mail you sent . . . " and she would be like, I have no idea of what you are talking about. And then the person would realize it was me. It's like, are you kidding?

OVERCOMING THE MICRO-INEQUITY OF ASSUMPTIONS, SLIGHTS, AND OTHER ANNOYANCES

While your antennae should be sensitive to disparate treatment, I caution against taking every comment or action too seriously. Try to focus on solutions to the problem and not someone's stupidity. Remember, sometimes our perceptions are not necessarily the objective reality. You don't want to cry wolf that you were discriminated against by someone who is an equal opportunity jerk. This diminishes your credibility as someone with good judgment who should be taken seriously. You will need this credibility if and when something truly egregious occurs.

John, the client I mentioned above, who brought the discrimination case because his boss would not say "hello" to him, wasted a lot of money and time because he was overly sensitive. While it was rude of his employer not to extend the common courtesy of "hello," John didn't realize that antidiscrimination laws are not civility codes. The laws do not protect against trivial slights and annoyances, per se.

A good strategy for testing the frequency of your antennae is having a group of colleagues and advisors who exercise good judgment and can keep your confidences. Before you allow a petty situation to ruin your work environment, ask your cadre of advisors for their thoughts. Depending on their expertise level, you should gather their advice for handling the situation. John's circle should have suggested that he find other ways to test whether his supervisor's "racist tendencies" were adversely affecting his employment or whether the supervisor was just inconsiderate. He could have put his supervisor in a position where he had to speak to him by asking questions related to a project or something very important in the workplace. Now, if the supervisor still did not speak to John, John would have a serious situation on his hands. His supervisor was not merely withholding salutations, but he would be affecting John's ability to do his job. If John was the only person of color in the department, and he was the only person the supervisor did not speak to, then John had a clearer case of discrimination. John would have had more evidence and information to make a serious complaint.

Be smart about dealing with subtle slights, assumptions, and other annoyances. When someone shows how in the dark he or she is about who you are, use it to your advantage. Don't get mad, get smart.

Paris* was a rising talent in her media firm. However, her supervisor thought that she was too young to get a particular promotion. Instead of getting angry, she turned the tables on his perceptions of youth.

> I was up for a promotion from manager to director, but the new president of my division thought I was too young to be a director. (I was in my mid-twenties and I have a youthful face.) He didn't give my boss the approval and told my boss that he thought I was too young, and that I needed to be more seasoned. Two weeks later at the company Christmas party the new president stopped to talk to me. He said, "I think you are around my daughter's age." I said, "Oh?" He said, "She's in her early thirties." I said with a smile, "Oh you're right. She is," knowing that I was only twenty-seven.
>
> My promotion was approved the next day.

CHAPTER TAKEAWAYS
- Although we have all been subjected to assumptions and slights, people of color, women, and some employees with disabilities are greater targets because they are hypervisible.
- Subtle slights and annoyances may seem minuscule, but they accumulate. Eventually, they build and may erode employee-employer relationships and eventually cause out-group employees to lose their loyalty to the organization.
- Subtle slights, annoyances, and assumptions are unnecessarily dangerous to an organization because they often lead to claims of discrimination and harassment.
- Research has found that our memories of negative experiences are more accurate than our memories of positive events. In fact, you need five good events to outweigh the negative physiological impact of a bad event.

CHAPTER 9
BEING THE FIRST AND HAVING AN EXTENSIVE NETWORK

I have a friend—I'll call him Albert*—who is incredibly smart and has great interpersonal skills. He graduated from top undergraduate and graduate schools and has worked for competitive companies. In essence, Albert, professionally, appears to be living the dream.

However, during a recent conversation with Albert, he explained the daunting complexities of advancing within his company that had nothing to do with merit or ability. He told me about a woman in his office who asked a senior-level executive for business development advice. She knocked on his door, sat down, and proceeded to ask the senior executive how he finds new business opportunities and generates million-dollar accounts for the company. The executive reached into his desk for a magazine. He pointed to the front cover of *Fortune* magazine and explained that his Aunt Sally, who was pictured next to a few well-known CEOs of Fortune 500s, creates introductions and access for him. This executive reached the highest level of success in this organization because he was able to pick up the telephone and ask his Aunt Sally to introduce him to any CEO he wanted to meet. What an enviable position!

Although Albert is bright, charismatic, personable, and courageous, he explained that as an African American male, his challenges in developing business were two-tiered. First, he did not feel welcomed enough by the executive or any of the White male executives in his office such that he could knock on their door to have a conversation about business development. Albert did not feel that he had the same access to a White male executive as his White female colleague did. He strongly doubted

139

whether the executive would be as open with him about business development. His second barrier to creating business the way the executive did was that he does not have an Aunt Sally or Uncle Sal with multimillion-dollar business connections. Albert is the first person in his family to work in a profession where he has to generate clients. So despite his hard work, Albert is forced to find other ways to demonstrate his value to his company because he does not think that he has lucrative connections at his fingertips.

The micro-inequity of being the first and having limited access to privilege is not uncommon for members of out-groups. Whether we are the first in our families to graduate from college, the first to pursue a career that requires an advanced degree, or the first generation to live in the United States, we realize that there are additional hurdles along the learning curve that slow down our advancement. Many of us realize that there is a point in our careers where our hard work will not get us as far as our connections. We observe how our counterparts in the majority often have an expansive network that works overtime for them. These networks, which are often created by their parents, get them into the best boarding schools, colleges, and companies. And once they are in these institutions, they have someone looking out for them. They have someone who cares about their development and their image and will steer them toward the best projects that will give them the best experience and best exposure. This is very powerful. Unlike our majority colleagues, we often do not have family members who are senior enough to make a telephone call on our behalf to recommend us for a position or convince a potential employer to meet with us for an interview. (Sometimes, even when we have connections we don't know how to use them to open doors for us.) To not have an extensive business network is like showing up to play in the major leagues but still having a T-ball bat. This is not to discount that employees with the privilege of having a second-generation advantage do not work hard. Sometimes, they work even harder as they prove that their success was hard won.

Sylvia Hong* understands all too well what it feels like to be denied access to a business network.

There's always a male club or a White club. When I was a partner in one of the large global New York firms, every partner had a III or IV after his name. There weren't too many female partners. The women partners usually worked harder and they didn't come from the same background as the men. Unless you went to prep school or had that type of family lineage—although you made partner—you were not part of the club. You didn't belong to the country club, you didn't go to prep school, you didn't go to Choate, you didn't go to Exeter, etc. You are always an outsider. It's always, they're entitled. It's their call as to how high you achieve in their game. You are not one of them. You're not invited to the same social gatherings; you don't have the same social background necessarily. You're not one of them. You never will be.

For the male side you weren't one of the guys unless you were into sports and other guy things. You don't get invited to do the social things, the after-work things where people continue to talk business. They had their own social circles. They would get together but I would never get invited. It made me feel like I wasn't one of them. Am I any different? No.

I left the firm in part because of this exclusion. No matter how hard I tried or how well I did, I was never going to be good enough to overcome that. And this was in every firm I worked at. Even in the government, if you're at the top you're either in the club or you're not. People generally hire alike. You have to want the diversity if you want to buck the trend. It's like the studies show, that if you have more "African American sounding first names" that are different than Michael or Jennifer, people look at the resumes differently. I just think that there are not many differences in firms or corporations unless they are global corporations where their business is driven globally, like a PepsiCo or Coke. But if they're not driven globally, if they don't have people from global groups, then it's not going to happen.

As the first, members of the out-groups often create their own path by walking it. We are the first in our families or group of friends to work in high-level professional environments. We are sometimes the first to sit at the same tables with dignitaries and other very important people you normally see on television. Sometimes, we're the ones on television. We don't have any family who are our in-the-home role models, or sources of information about how to develop business strategies, deal with a disorganized supervisor, or any of the other higher-tiered maladies of the workplace. We have to go it alone. Just when we thought that that our Master's, Juris Doctor, or Doctor of Medicine degree was making life easier, the ride has just begun. For many different reasons, we may be the first.

When Keith Clarkson* looks back to the earlier days of his career, he quickly runs out of fingers to count the number of mistakes and missteps he made. Keith finally made it to the partnership ranks of his firm, but it was a struggle. Even as a White male, he felt left out of influential networks that could have assisted him in his career.

> I grew up lower-middle class in a small suburb of Cleveland and nobody else on either side of my family was an attorney. Even though my dad was a school superintendent and had a PhD in education and I had one uncle who had a PhD and was a professor of biology, no one else in my family had graduate degrees. From the standpoint of having input, and models and familiarity with what attorneys do, what career paths, what credentials matter, how to network, how to draw business, and any of that stuff, I did not have a built-in model from my upbringing. I went to New York University, which had a pretty good career services counseling division, but I still didn't feel like I learned and understood a lot of things that I believe people with a different upbringing would naturally know. If I had had such a background, I might have made wiser choices that would have increased my flexibility earlier in my career.
>
> In terms of interviewing, developing mentoring relationships, and things like that, my perception is that people generally subconsciously find it easier to relate to people who share more characteristics with them. While I did not feel like I had as acute of a set of differences in my background—the way I talked, the way I dressed, and my understanding of things and my interests—as people

with legally protected characteristics, I had enough of a difference that there were instances that I felt caused me to not get the job or to not be mentored as much as someone else.

Now that I am on the flip side of the situation and in a position to mentor others, I try to make sure that I'm not limiting the extent to which I extend myself and recognize capability and encourage development in other people based on focusing on my ability to feel comfortable with them given my own unique set of things that make me who I am. I've never had anything horrible happen to me. I feel like everyone, except the ultra-privileged, have felt like outsiders at times and sometimes it has adversely affected them because of people's tendency to fall back on going with what is most familiar and comfortable to them.

In addition to being the first in her family to become an anesthesiologist, Barbara Tomlinson* feels that she has to figure out how to do her job without the support of her colleagues. She works in a community hospital affiliate of a prestigious university. This is the first time where she is working in an institution where the staff comprises ethnic and racial minorities to a considerable degree to the point where Caucasians may be in the numerical minority in her department. Yet she still feels like an outsider in many instances. She is one of the youngest attendings on staff, so she is a minority in terms of her age. In terms of experience, this is her third year out of residency, so she is essentially the third least experienced physician on staff. So those two factors should set her apart for informal mentoring, but they do not.

I find that, particularly, when I interact with surgeons I feel like an outsider. There have been many instances where I am not invited to join in on the camaraderie that exists between some of the more established attendings and surgeons. It's like my focus is basically to come in and do the job that I was hired to do. The interactions that occur within the hospital setting tend to be about business with me while they tend to be more social chit-chat when occurring amongst other people. I don't know if it extends to socializing outside of work, because if it does then I am totally unaware of it. That is how out of the loop I am.

Within even the most transparent workplace networks, there are power dynamics and a culture of respecting the power dynamic. Those who are outside of the workplace network often do not know the unwritten rules and protocol of how to navigate the network. Ambitious professionals like Carter Jefferson* learn through painful trial and error how to respect the power dynamic's elusive culture.

Carter works for an international media company, and he recently had his first encounter with the power dynamic.

A great example of what's going on in my current job is who's on the leadership track and who's not. And it's a little bit hot and cold. Now it's about not hearing about things. Like, all of a sudden someone is in a new role and you never even knew about it. No one pulled you to the side and gave you the opportunity to consider it.

Someone from corporate had put my name in the hat for a leadership program at a historically Black college where I would be an adjunct faculty person for a day. It was a part of a broader initiative. They sent me this formal letter and asked me to consider it. I was excited about it. I decided to forward the information to my boss and my boss's boss and let them know that I was chosen by the executive team to do this. There was zero response via e-mail. So my wheels are turning. What ended up happening was that I ran into the person from corporate who sent me the e-mail and he said that he had his hand slapped the other day. I said, "What you are talking about?" He said, "I had selected you because you've done a lot of things for corporate. You've spoken on panels and done a lot of things. But the head of HR for my division contacted the HR person in corporate and said, 'I pick my people, you don't pick my people. So if you want someone from my division in on that leadership program, I pick those people; you don't.'" So it was a power play.

Once again, it's an issue of who is in your inner circle and who is not. I didn't get the nod from the head of HR from my division because I had not befriended that person. There are favorites. There are people who are picked for the short list for leadership development, for visible projects at any organization. And the favorites tend to get shaped by what's familiar, like who you hang out with, etc. It's not from a meritocracy standpoint. Who is in your inner circle? You take care of the folks who are around you. Sometimes we have to extend ourselves, in unreasonable ways, to become a part of the network, but it doesn't mean that we are a part of the network in a real way. It's a chess game.

Judy Tabar is the executive director of Planned Parenthood of Southern New England (PPSNE) who appreciates the privileges that traveled with her throughout life. She started her career in medicine in 1973 as one of the first women in the Physician Assistant (PA) program at the University of Iowa Medical School. At the time, the PA degree was a new career to the medical profession and had only been in existence since 1968. When she arrived at her first assignment to meet with patients, the staff gave her a filing assignment. She had to really convince people that she had the skills and was legitimate. It is a testament to her good-nature that she is able to laugh about going to medical school only to be given filing. When she later joined PPSNE, she was determined to create a diverse and inclusive organization, both for the staff and for the clients.

I was a leader learning how to create that environment, and I learned from my staff. For example, a number of staff of color who aspired to move up within the organization were always impeccably dressed above what was really the norm in the organization at the time. I was impressed and surprised by that. I learned from them that their culture and their families told them that if they wanted to get ahead they would confront some barriers and that they would have to rise above everyone else. I had not put two and two together until a member of my staff told me about the incredible pressures that they felt to be a cut above and be better than everyone else. I felt sad that they felt that much pressure. As a result of this enlightenment we had a number of conversations as we continued our journey to be a more diverse and inclusive organization. It really created empathy within the organization and created an understanding of the different backgrounds and perspectives that we bring into the workplace that are not visible to others.

I think when one takes that route of thinking that the *twice as good* syndrome is paranoia, you're not understanding the experience of the other person. For me, it's the invisible becoming visible and honoring and valuing that experience. I also think about the experience that my African American staff members told me about *driving while Black*. I think about the injustice and that when I was teaching my son how to drive, I never thought about him getting unlawfully stopped by the police. There is no doubt in my mind that what I was hearing was real.

As the leader of an organization that serves the needs of young men and women of all different backgrounds, if we are truly going to serve them well, we need to understand all their perspectives and we need to be a welcoming place for anyone who walks through our doors. It has been imperative for us to learn and understand all of the cultural differences. And this applies to all levels of the organization—from the board level to the staff level to the clinician level. It has been both a business imperative and a social justice imperative.

I remember one of my board members and I went to a three-day diversity workshop event. We were seeking to learn more about how to diversify our organization, and a lot of that involved better understanding of our own and others' experiences.

My board member and I participated in this activity where we all stood in a line and the facilitator would ask us to take one step forward for various things, like if you had more than ten books in your house, or take one step back if you didn't. My board member was an African American woman with a master's degree in social work. By the end of these questions I was almost at the front of the room and she was still in the back of the room. I came from a middle-class family and neither of my parents went to college. My board member was from a better educated background than I and yet the advantages I had over the barriers that she experienced were just exemplified in space. She said to me, "My mother worked so hard for me to get to the head of the room and look, I'm still in the back of the room."

ERADICATING THE BARRIER OF BEING THE FIRST

One of the best quotes about the responsibility and accountability of being a trailblazer comes from Elaine T. Jones, former executive director of the NAACP Legal Defense Fund. She said, "The job of the first is to keep the door open for others. If when you leave things haven't changed, then you have not done what you were supposed to do." Bernice Washington is a rare gem who lives this quote. She is from a small town in Louisiana and was the first in her family to land a senior-level position in pharmaceutical sales. Most people would step away from their values and morals in exchange for the high-stakes rewards of pharmaceutical sales. Yet, Bernice saw her role and her purpose as the first as having more significance.

Although I may have the same or better education than my colleagues, my performance may be superior to theirs, but still I am not considered for the same opportunities. Many decision makers make selections for positions based on *their* compatibility with individuals rather than capability. That observation and experience has freed me up to be a change agent. I feel I was born to kick doors open for others, understanding that I would not be the one to walk through them. My children are prepared and are walking through doors that I know I help kick open. Sometimes it's not in your lifetime that you will see or reap the benefits of the opportunities that you create for others. I am a big proponent of women being promoted and being in positions of power and authority. I challenged the organizational chart and management team makeup in any organization with whom I am associated. The question has always been, why are there few or no women and why there are few or no minorities in senior-level positions? Those are the sort of questions that leadership prefers not be asked. Not only do I ask them, but I ask them at public forums where decision makers can hear them and others can help hold them accountable for their response. If there are twenty-four executives on the platform and all of them are White men, then the question is legitimate. Many still do not see anything wrong with that picture. I know that pushing that hard, I would never be the beneficiary of any resulting changes.

Then months later, there were women, African Americans, and Hispanics promoted to major positions. Many credit my challenging the status quo for the organizational changes. I knew strategically that the executives could not refute the lack of and need for diversity, especially since I supported my arguments with statistics about the marketplace. X percent of the people buying their products were women and X percent of them were African American and Hispanic. With that kind of data it became difficult to argue against diversity. My arguments were based on statistics and market share. That's how you change things—not by screaming and other nonsense. Provide data and facts that they can't refute and get some people to raise a little hell. That's the shortcut to lasting change.

Anyone who has been to college knows that there is more to college than homework. At four-year colleges, students who are the first in their families to attend college are twice as likely as their counterparts who have at least one parent with a bachelor's degree to drop out of college by their first year.[51]

Immediately after my first year of law school, I found the most valuable document I would ever receive in law school that a professor had thoughtfully slipped into my mailbox. Professor Raymond Diamond always seemed aloof to me. He would say a quick "hello" if we passed each other in the hallway, but we never really stopped to talk. I did not know him very well, but he most likely knew where I was coming from. Similar to 95 percent of my African American classmates, I was the first in my family to attend law school and I had no idea of what I was doing. I'm sure that Professor Diamond suspected that. He created a succinct outline of the types of opportunities 1Ls (first-year law students) should pursue during the summer before their second year of law school. Initially, I thought my friends on law review were underachievers for aggressively pursuing unpaid judicial clerkships. My thinking was, who can afford to work for free after accumulating law school debt? However, Professor Diamond's one-sheeter explained the value of a judicial clerkship in terms that the Career Services Office did not possess. (While I am sure that this same information was in a book on legal careers, who had time to read anything that was not related to class?) Similar to Professor Diamond's one-sheeter, colleges and universities could create a snapshot of the plum fellowships, clerkships, and other competitive programs that are usually privy only to a privileged few. Within organizations, a one-sheeter about career mapping could be used to support any professional development programming that is offered. The goal of the one-sheeter is to give the firsts the answers to questions they didn't even know they had.

Gilbert Casellas found himself trying to figure out removing this micro-inequity when he was general counsel of the US Air Force during President Clinton's administration.

The military is a little more challenging just because there is this perception that it is all merit based in that you can measure quantitatively the issue of merit however it is defined. And in some cases you can certainly measure performance looking at who does this and who does that better, that is to say, looking at certain situations and criteria quantitatively. The problem is that as you move up the ranks, there's a lot of qualitative judgment made that affects the ability to be ready for those ostensibly quantitative measures.

This was one of the things that I discovered when I was at the Department of the Air Force. At that time the secretary of the air force, my boss, was the first female service secretary and was very committed to identifying barriers and eliminating them not just with regard to women and female pilots, for example, but in regard to all the various jobs that exist in the air force for everyone.

One of the things we saw when it came to promotions in the medical profession, for example, within the Air Force, was the importance of professional certifications. For example, doctors get certified into, for example, the American College of Surgeons or Radiology, etc. Hence, you are deemed a specialist in your profession and are designated as such. We were finding that minority officers who were coming up in that promotion pool of medical professionals did not have those professional certifications and therefore when stacked up against majority candidates, who had those credentials, obviously did not stack up well. So the question was, are there barriers that led to that situation, unconscious or otherwise? Are there things that we're doing as a service that prevent folks from getting there? Is there informal mentoring that could help someone know, for example, that that's the kind of thing that you need to do? It's not unlike informal mentoring in the traditional corporate law firm where a senior person has been at a firm, knows the culture, knows the personalities, and mentors someone junior, advising "Listen, when you deal with X partner, just keep this in mind or approach him a certain way." Those unwritten rules that come with an informal mentor can determine whether your career gets derailed or not. In some ways I don't think it's that different in these other settings. I think it just manifests itself differently in different settings.

In our work on the MLDC (Military Leadership Diversity Committee), the issues were not unlike those in Corporate America when you look at the senior leadership. You find a dearth of diverse representation at the top. And the question is, why is that? The military is unique in that you can't go out and recruit somebody to be a three- or four-star general. You have to grow your generals, and it takes like thirty years to grow them. So you're basically starting at the top of a funnel with several hundred individuals, and over the course of time you may end up with one who makes it to the general or flag officer level.

Six years ago, when I wrote my last book, most organizations made the mistake of not pumping many resources into their affinity groups or employee resource groups (ERGs), assuming that they could run on automatic pilot. Around the same time, Harvard Professor Frank Dobbins's research, *Best Practices or Best Guesses? Assessing the Efficacy of Corporate Affirmative Action and Diversity Policies*, found that affinity groups more often than not fail to create meaningful networks for minority employees and do not advance diversity because they are comprised of junior-level employees with minimal experience with and influence over the organization. Fortunately, a lot has changed since then.

More and more companies and organizations have found value in their ERGs, from their test marketing capabilities to their potential to foster morale and inclusion in the workplace. In terms of helping "the firsts" build a sense of community, they have been used to assist with the hiring and onboarding process. (Although there is some debate that it is impossible to be "the first" when there is an ERG, I use the term "the first" from the individual's perspective. While there might be other members of your demographic group in your organization, you may still be the first in your family or social group to attain a certain level of success in a particular industry.) At a recent "Diversity Breakfast" in Connecticut, the vice president of diversity for ESPN shared that as a Puerto Rican, before she took the job (based in rural Bristol, Connecticut) she called and spoke with ESPN employees about where to shop for Puerto Rican food. Many organizations leverage their ERGs by having their members talk to candidates during the hiring process.

While not all companies and organizations have figured out how to maximize their ERGs, I have shown many how to create partnerships on career management, leadership skills building, and the other initiatives that are needed to become effective leaders.

OVERCOMING THE BARRIER OF BEING THE FIRST

During the 2013 National Conference on Race and Ethnicity (NCORE), I was wowed by many speakers. There was Melissa Harris-Perry of MSNBC, the author and race thought leader Tim Wise, and Damon Williams of the University of Wisconsin. One of the most powerful sessions was from Kerry Ann Rockquemore, PhD. Although she looks like an undergraduate, she was a highly successful tenured professor who figured out what was holding back many professors of color from reaching tenure—lack of a supportive network. She founded the National Center for Faculty Development & Diversity, which she describes as an "independent professional development, training, and mentoring community of over 25,000 graduate students, post-docs, and faculty members." She built a network of professors and other academic experts to provide a community of support for aspiring professors who have weak networks. She found that many professors of color were relying on the wrong people or were not relying on anyone. As she eloquently put it, "Unless your momma is the provost, you need to build a better network." The chart on the next page is a good example of how she forces members of the NCFD to visualize their networks so that they can identify the weaknesses and strengths. Regardless of your company's formal mentoring program, corporate university, or any other leadership program, your career development is your responsibility. It is up to you to take charge of where you want to go and how you are going to get there.

The first step for gaining access to a network is to be a stellar performer. When your work speaks for itself, others will recognize you and want to learn more about you.

You should also devote a percentage of your time to networking and meeting more people. Obviously, the more people you know, the more access you have to information, resources, and opportunities. Networking is a two-way street. The worst networkers are the people who only promote themselves and do not think about how they can help others. Just think, do you enjoy being in a conversation with someone who only talks about him or herself? Try to start the conversation by asking what the next person does, and really listen and seem interested. The more you know about the next person, the better positioned you are to figure out how you fit within each other's lives.

Once you actually make connections with new people, you need to follow up. One of my favorite business principles from *Nice Girls Don't Get the Corner Office: 101 Unconscious Mistakes Women Make That Sabotage Their Careers* (Lois P. Frankel, 2005) is, "When you need that relationship, it's already too late to build it." I'll admit, when I was a law student I found the follow-up aspect of networking challenging. I was good at meeting people, carrying on a great conversation, and then it would end there. I would get caught up with a paper for school and would forget to e-mail or send the person I met a "nice to meet you" card.

Here's a good example of how I cheated myself of a friendship with a US Senator. When I was in law school, an unassuming affable attorney conducted a mock interview session with me. He coached me through

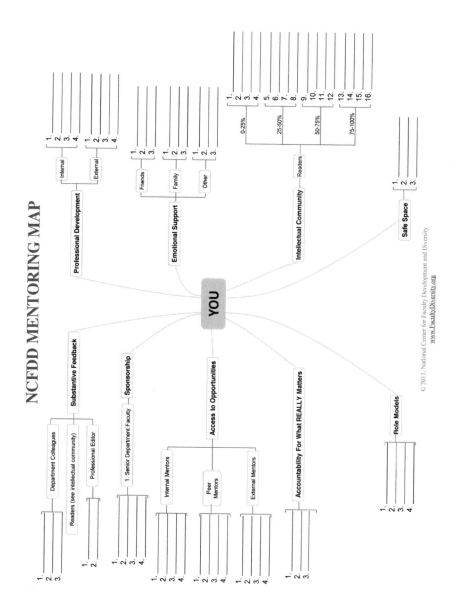

NCFDD MENTORING MAP

Professional Development
- Internal
  1.
  2.
  3.
  4.
- External
  1.
  2.
  3.
  4.

Emotional Support
- Friends
  1.
  2.
  3.
- Family
  1.
  2.
  3.
- Other
  1.
  2.
  3.

Intellectual Community
- Readers
  1.
  2.
  3.
  4.
  - 0-25%
  5.
  6.
  7.
  8.
  - 25-50%
  9.
  10.
  11.
  12.
  - 50-75%
  13.
  14.
  15.
  16.
  - 75-100%

Safe Space
1.
2.
3.

YOU

Substantive Feedback
- Department Colleagues
  1.
  2.
  3.
- Readers (see intellectual community)
- Professional Editor
  1.
  2.

Sponsorship
1. Senior Department Faculty
  1.
  2.
  3.
  4.

Access to Opportunities
- Internal Mentors
  1.
  2.
  3.
  4.
- Peer Mentors
  1.
  2.
  3.
  4.
- External Mentors
  1.
  2.
  3.
  4.

Accountability For What REALLY Matters
1.
2.
3.

Role Models
1.
2.
3.
4.

answering questions to any future employer's satisfaction. He encouraged me to keep in touch. Between looking for a summer clerkship and trying to keep up with reading for class, I never followed up. I didn't send a thank-you note or an e-mail after the mock interview session. Six months later, I picked up my Sunday newspaper and learned that this unassuming attorney, David Vitter, was running for the Senate. I was elated when he won, but I couldn't resist the urge to kick myself for not staying in touch.

Meeting new people and creating meaningful new relationships takes practice and time. You may have to meet some people a few times before you actually click. With mobile device technologies like smartphones and PDAs, there are fewer excuses for not staying in touch. Many times, I will send someone I just met a quick e-mail when I am on the train or I will immediately schedule a telephone call with a person I want to meet with for lunch. Each month I write a quick e-newsletter and send it to everyone I know, which is a lot easier than sending 2,500 e-mails to the colleagues, clients, and friends in my database. Today, I designate at least 30 percent of my time to meeting and keeping in touch with the people I meet. Truly, there is no point in collecting cards if you are not going to use this information wisely.

One of my favorite training programs that I present to professional trade organizations, such as the National Black MBAs, is "Finding Your Office Rabbi." While mentors can assist with procedural and substantive work-related issues, rabbis are a whole other area of support. Rabbis in Judaism are more than spiritual leaders. Since they know everyone in the congregation, they are great sources of information. They know about real estate, they know about financial investments, and they even know who is single and make for great matchmakers. Rabbis provide resources that help their congregants navigate through life's most tricky areas.

Similarly, a workplace rabbi or a sponsor is just as pivotal to one's workplace success. More than a mentor, he or she can open doors when merit and hard work cannot. Workplace rabbis advocate for you when you are not present in meetings. They mention your work to important people. And they introduce you to the people you need to know. Although Albert did not have a biological Aunt Sally, he could have adopted such an aunt. He should have mined his alumni database to cultivate the relationships that could have eventually led to a great connection. A great example of how important it is to have someone looking out for you was presented in a *New York Times* article, "Under 40, Successful, and Itching for a New Career."[52] The article featured an attractive blonde woman who was able to move from Omaha, Nebraska, to New York, land a great job, attend parties where she could meet partners of major New York City law firms, and get set up on a blind date with an oncologist because she had a rabbi. Her rabbi introduced her to a network of people who cared about her personal and professional well-being. Within a year, she had access to privileged circles that most people who spend their entire lives in New York do not have.

CHAPTER TAKEAWAYS

- When one takes that route of thinking that the *twice as good* syndrome is paranoia, you're not understanding the experience of the other person.
- Within organizations, a one-sheeter about career mapping could be used to support any professional development programming that is offered. The goal of the one-sheeter is to give "the firsts" the answers to questions they didn't even know they had.
- As you move up the ranks there is a lot of qualitative judgment made that affects the ability to be ready for those ostensibly quantitative measures.
- If you do not have a biological Aunt Sally who is well connected and can open doors for you, adopt one.

CHAPTER 10
ISOLATION AND FEELING INVISIBLE

The leaky pipeline, the sticky floor, and the attrition dilemma are often used to describe the phenomena where organizational diversity disappears the higher you climb the organizational ladder. In 2010, US Senator Robert Menendez (D-NJ) conducted a study of the Fortune 500 companies and found that minorities represent only 10.44 percent of executive managers, and although women make up half of the workforce, they represent 19.87 percent of directors.[53] (Gay and transgender employees make up about 6 percent of the workforce, while people with disabilities make up only 21 percent of the workforce.)[54]

There are myriad reasons to explain the dearth of women and minorities in management positions. By the time professionals who were the "only one" could have advanced to senior management, many had already left the company because of the horrible experiences of being excluded. Some leave because they grew tired of watching others with fewer qualifications get the better assignments, or they grew tired of getting edged out for promotions. Even worse, some were asked to leave.

> "I am invisible, understand, simply because people refuse to see me. Like the bodiless heads you see sometimes in circus sideshows, it is as though I have been surrounded by mirrors of hard, distorting glass. When they approach me they see only my surroundings, themselves, or figments of their imagination—indeed, everything and anything except me."
>
> —Ralph Ellison, *Invisible Man*

An aspect of being an outsider is being and feeling alone. Because you do not have any or many others who share important characteristics and experiences with you, you can feel ostracized from conversations and not privy to the collegiality of the group. The micro-inequity of feeling isolated directly impacts our social needs and sense of belonging within Mazlow's hierarchy of needs. Being the "only one" increases the chances of feeling invisible. When we are not a part of the social fabric in an organization, it is not difficult to feel excluded. As I mentioned, being seen and heard in formal and informal settings is crucial for career advancement.

Raheema Strickland* was a young Black associate in a law firm with 1,000 lawyers and a handful of associates of color when she had to leap out of her comfort zone. She was often the only brown face in a room and the only voice of color in a conversation. Something as simple as starting and joining a conversation was a challenge for Raheema.

When I was a summer associate at a large New York City law firm, I felt like sometimes when you would get in conversations with people, either groups of other lawyers or groups of other partners and summers where they would start talking about something, I had no relation to them. I don't know if it was class or race. I can't clearly identify what it was. It just seemed like we had very different experiences. Whatever it was that they were discussing, I just didn't feel like I could contribute to the conversation. So I would just find another group of people to talk to. After a while, I started inserting whatever my experiences or opinions were even if I couldn't relate to what they were talking about.

Raheema knew that she could not afford to be a quiet minority in her firm. She had to find a way to display her gregarious personality and be a visible part of the group.

Sometimes those in the majority are so unfamiliar with "your type" that they do not know how to relate to you. Many people are not curious or courageous enough to leave their comfort zones to find out about someone—in a respectful way—who they suspect is different from them. Some people in the majority are afraid that they may say or do something offensive. Some may just assume that they have nothing in common with a person in the minority and thus nothing to say. It is not uncommon for those in the majority to do what feels easy and comfortable: socialize with the people who look like and act like them.

Kahleel Faroud* saw his career in the financial services industry slipping off-track when he was hired as an investment banking firm's first and only Muslim. The novelty of being the first had consequences Kahleel did not anticipate.

I felt like I was the only person of color when I worked in private banking. The person who hired me did not treat me any different than my coworkers. The team that I was placed on, well, I felt a little bit outside of my comfort zone.

We had different ethnicities and at the same time different religious beliefs as well. Although we didn't speak about it, there were other team members that shared the same ethnicities and the same religious backgrounds, and I just felt like they bonded more so with each other than with me. I just didn't feel comfortable in terms of asking questions or being invited to certain outings. I'm Muslim and these gentlemen were Jewish. They were pro-Israel and I am from Afghanistan.

In the beginning when I was hired what was unique was that they invited me to join the team, but once I joined the team I noticed that I wasn't being trained. That was a little bit strange to me. I don't know what the dynamics or the selection criteria were for the group to invite me to the team and then not give me the resources and training to be successful. There was a training program. After you obtain your licenses, you are absorbed into a private wealth team. Usually, you shadow the senior wealth managers on client calls at various meetings. The only client call that I ever attended was a lead that I was able to bring to the table, whereas in other situations the trainees were able to go to client calls when they didn't source that opportunity themselves. That's something I did not understand. I was not given any feedback, so basically I had to learn on my own while others were being taken under the wings of senior people and being shown how to create asset allocation models. I was given limited guidance where I could have easily made mistakes that could jeopardize my licenses or give an investment idea that was not suitable for the client.

The members of my group, one colleague and the person who ran the team, basically my supervisor, liked to play tennis. I like to play tennis occasionally. They would talk about instances where they would go play tennis, yet they never invited me. Even regular greetings in the morning where after you develop a relationship with someone you talk a bit more casually. You talk about the weekend, sports, etc. They were always very professional with me. They just usually said good morning to me. I attempted numerous times to develop relationships, but I could see it was not welcomed.

I really left because there was a better opportunity where I am now. Today, I work for a nonprofit organization that trains and develops students of color who want to pursue careers in banking. At the same time the reason why I was seeking a new opportunity was because I just felt like the hurdle was not set for success; it was set for failure. Once I saw that the outcome of working there was not too bright, I started looking for other opportunities. My current position just fell in my lap. Had it not been for feeling like I was not getting trained or was not feeling welcomed in the team, I probably would have stayed in private banking and not looked for other opportunities. I stayed with the company for eight or nine months. It took me about two months to get my licenses, and then the other six months I was placed on a team. Then it became evident that it was not a good fit during the fourth month. I spoke with the woman who hired me and voiced my concern and she was very busy and basically told me to figure it out. But when I went back to the team, the dynamic was not there. Then it started getting really uncomfortable. There was never a conflict. It never got to that point.

Tamika Lewiston* saw similar signs of sabotage to her career as a chemist. When she joined her company, she could not help but think, "It is 2007. Why am I the only Black chemist in this company?" After a few years of traversing the bumpy and arduous terrain as the only Black person in her company, she understood why and left for higher ground.

> There were a couple of instances where I was not copied on a couple of e-mails for test results and instrumentation. When the vice president specifically asked for test results, I just stood there with my mouth open because I was not copied on the original e-mail from the boss, who was Puerto Rican. I tried to talk to the boss but she wasn't too responsive. So I figured that I would have a closed-door meeting with her. It turned into a confrontation instead of a conversation. She denied that she left me out of the loop and she denied that she did not copy me on the e-mail. I felt like I wasn't even a part of the group. I felt like I didn't have a voice. I left that job in part because I felt like an outsider.
>
> The big difference in the previous job and my current job is that there are a lot more minorities in my department in general. When I was first hired, I was the only full-time woman, but I wasn't the only Black person. We had a lot of diversity. We had a Jamaican man and a Vietnamese woman. Through the years we got a Russian man, we got another woman who was half Vietnamese and half Cambodian. We have a guy who is from the Dominican Republic. We have a guy from Scotland. We have a guy who is Filipino and a Chinese man. And that's just a handful of our diversity, and that makes a big difference. You don't feel as ostracized because of your race because there is a lot of diversity. The boss that I had when I first was hired, he never saw color or sex. I just happened to be the only woman by chance. He always focused on who was the most qualified.

ERADICATING THE MICRO-INEQUITY OF ISOLATION

Recruitment is probably the number one strategy an organization can use to increase the diversity of the staff and organizational leadership. Savvy organizations have figured out creative recruitment strategies, such as attending (and sponsoring) career fairs that attract prospective employees of color, women, Latinos, and the LGBT community. Organizations have also engaged in very aggressive (and expensive) advertising campaigns and sponsor events to assist with their recruitment strategies. These are safe approaches, but do they really maximize the organization's ability to market itself to diverse communities? How much impact does sponsoring an award's banquet or placing an advertisement in a magazine have on a candidate who walks through your organization and sees that he or she will be the only one in a particular department?

Instead, organizations could develop or sponsor programs that give students tangible employment skills and create a real impact on the lives of future employees. For instance, for Black History Month, I worked with White & Case, an international law firm, in presenting a seminar about career fulfillment for Columbia Law School's Black Law Student Association. In an informal setting, but within a purpose-driven conversation, the students had an opportunity to hear about life at the law firm as it related to their career goals. The conversation definitely went beyond the law firm's brochure. The attorneys provided insight as to how they navigated their careers and made different decisions that often stump people when they enter the workplace. The students walked away feeling empowered with new information and felt less mind-blind. White & Case's profile was significantly elevated in the Black law students' minds because they saw that the firm cared about their professional development regardless of where they decided to work. It was not just another networking event. These are the types of programs that truly show an investment in and attract diverse candidates.

Organizations should meaningfully look to their employees for referrals for filling job openings and to participate in interviews and selection committees.

Harvey Benitez* not only participates in his firm's hiring and selection committee but his presence also sets the tone for changing the firm's dangerous misperceptions about candidates of color.

Being a Latino lawyer it's difficult to interact with other Latinos or get qualified Latino candidates to be taken seriously. I am the sole Latino at my firm. There's just a sense in the Pacific Northwest, which is where I practice, that there just isn't a real effort to bring any critical mass of people together. I think the primary way

I feel like an outsider is not having any Latino peers, and when I do bring in qualified outstanding people of color they don't really get a chance. It is inordinately difficult to get attorneys of color hired. The firm says that it is looking for qualified candidates, and when I do find them qualified candidates it always seems like there's a reason to not hire them: it's too late in the season, the candidate's grades aren't good, or the firm has already looked at other folks. The firm may bring people in for a screening interview, but that's it.

We have diversity speakers come into town, and there was a Latino speaker and I was sitting at a table with people who were on the managing committee for the firm. I had a curious episode with a partner who was on the executive committee for the firm. His experience was that some minority groups, like Latinos, don't like to work at law firms or work at, what I consider, good jobs for their futures. I found that that was the attitude. I told him that in my experiences, all kinds of law students from diverse backgrounds try to seek high-paying jobs that look good on their resumes and that will open jobs for their futures. He did not have a response.

This made me feel like on some level there may have been good intentions but, especially with recruiting, the good intentions don't reflect in making good recruiting or lateral decisions. Even though people say they are interested in diversity, when I've brought specific people to the firm's attention, these candidates have not gotten a fair shake. It's frustrating. It doesn't make me feel like I have a long-term future with the firm. I think that the firm tries to bring in diverse folks but they aren't taking all of the necessary steps to really make a change or a significant difference. The firm should be making sure that when people are available who are of diverse backgrounds that the firm makes a special effort to go get them, as opposed to having some other reason or excuse why they are not a good fit. Mostly in the recruiting part, that feels frustrating.

Organizations that feel as though there are not enough diverse candidates to choose from could also be a part of the process for changing the situation and increasing the pipeline of diverse candidates. There are so many opportunities for organizations to create a presence in underserved communities with a minimal time commitment. For organizations that claim that they do not have the time or the resources to coordinate pipeline efforts, I would encourage you to create a community service officer position in your organization. This person would be tasked with organizing all of your organization's outreach efforts. In the alternative, consider hiring consulting firms, to coordinate and manage your community service and pipeline programs. For instance, my firm created a weekly career exploration series with the Minisink Townhouse, an inner-city recreation center, and the New York City Bar Association's Young Lawyer's Committee, which brought together professionals with a wealth of life advice and young people who were eager to hear it. The only role the City Bar played was providing volunteers and notifying them of the one-hour volunteer sessions. That's right, an organization can help thousands of students a year by investing just one hour of time per person.

OVERCOMING THE MICRO-INEQUITY OF ISOLATION

The employees who make some of the best career decisions are the ones who did their homework about the company. If you are planning to work for an organization that has no or few minorities, try to ask as many questions as possible. Ask your school career counselor if he or she knows anything about this company, or if they can connect you to graduates who worked for the organization. Don't be shy about reaching out to your school alumni base and the local professional trade associations, especially those that focus on underrepresented groups.

Sometimes, there are benefits to being one of a few raisins in the bread pudding. While I am hard pressed to accept the corporate excuse, "we can't find any," racial minorities do tend to cluster in cities, leaving a wide expanse of Midwestern states that have very low percentages of people of color. During a provocative presentation by a diversity manager of a major health care organization, she provided compelling data for relocating and reconsidering your profession. According to Gallup's 2012 employment poll and index, the following states had the highest levels of job growth:[55]

1. North Dakota
2. South Dakota
3. Nebraska
4. Washington, DC
5. Iowa
6. Texas
7. Minnesota
8. Indiana
9. Oklahoma
10. Utah

Yet, according to the 2010 US Census, the following states had the highest percentages of racial diversity (the following are not in order):[56]

1. Hawaii
2. Georgia
3. Washington, DC
4. Arizona
5. California
6. New York
7. New Jersey
8. Nevada
9. Texas
10. Florida

Of the states with the highest percentage of racial minorities, only Texas and Washington, DC, also appeared on the list of states with the highest job growth. The diversity manager gave a few case studies of individuals of color who decided to brave isolation and moved to states and cities with job growth. Because they are the "only one" and hypervisible, they are often tapped for opportunities and have access to political and business leaders who are eager to support diversity.

Although there is comfort in numbers, you shouldn't be afraid to be the "only one." You may be the only one because you are in a highly specialized area where there aren't too many people of any background.

Period. Ultimately, your attitude and perspective about the environment will influence your experience as the only one.

For instance, Edward Rodriquez* and Luz Costa* had completely different experiences being the only employees from working-class backgrounds working among privileged employees. Edward found that he was not only one of a handful of Filipinos in his investment banking firm but he was also one of the few who came from a different socioeconomic background. Because of his attitude, he could never feel comfortable in his firm.

> I think a lot of what I encountered in the workplace were very subtle forms of racism, but my experience was more about diversity in thought, and diversity not being appreciated in terms of socioeconomic status. I grew up in a low-income urban neighborhood. The majority of my coworkers, even those who were of color, didn't necessarily have my background. I felt like such a minority. I was the one who came from a background where I felt like I struggled to get to a place like Morgan Stanley that has a lot of the trappings of success and a lot of the privileges that come with being around a lot of money—and that always made me feel uncomfortable. And it still does.

Luz Costa, on the other hand, determined that as long as she worked in an environment that was respectful and offered equal opportunities, her unfamiliarity with the financial trappings of her new environment would not ensnarl her career development.

> The only difference between my colleagues and me was that I came from very humble means. I've had to work my way up. In my first firm, there were a lot of people with a lot of wealth. Going to a cocktail party or the firm's summer outing or something like that, I saw that wealth and felt a little in awe of it, like "Wow, there's so much money in this room; look at this fantastic multimillion-dollar pad in Manhattan, it's amazing." Once you see it for the first time, you move on. We're human beings; it doesn't matter what the differences are in terms of socioeconomic backgrounds. It was not uncomfortable

for me because people around me made me comfortable. You get past the wealth differences very quickly because the people I worked and socialized with were great human beings. To this day, I am still in touch with those folks from my first firm who were very wealthy, so we bridged any differences or the differences were irrelevant. There's one guy in particular who comes from a very wealthy family and we e-mail each other occasionally about going to a basketball game together with our kids. Those barriers did not get in the way of friendships or other relationships, professional or otherwise. That was my experience. I can't tell you that we became close friends, but relationships did happen notwithstanding those differences.

I've only had two jobs professionally: one at a law firm and one at a consulting firm. At both of those places I have felt very comfortable, actually, as a woman. I never had an issue gender-wise. I also felt very comfortable race-wise. I never felt uncomfortable because I was perhaps the only Hispanic in the room. Everybody around me was so professional and so attuned to diversity that it was not an issue at all. People were extremely supportive in every way.

Lerleen Boudreaux* is another junior-level professional who refuses to allow any other characteristic that could make her an outsider to get in the way of her career. When she made the move from a small farm in Illinois to New York City, she was thrust into an entirely different lifestyle. While her colleagues talk about growing up in apartments and their boarding school experiences, she thinks twice about whether she wants to talk about milking cows and taking care of farm animals. In addition to her rural upbringing, being a woman at times has its challenges, but it has never stood in her way.

Sometimes it's odd to be the only woman in a meeting with ten or twelve men. I can't think of a specific instance where I was offended, but I do encounter investment banker mentalities. You know, the jocular references. For instance, they use terms like "open kimono" when you're discussing open disclosure of documents. I'm not offended by any of this because it's part of the environment. You can't be so thin-skinned that you're always offended. There have been some instances where I have felt excluded, but it was never anything horrible or blatant. I have never encountered anything that I have not been able to finesse.

Remember Susan de las Cuevas* and how she used her employer's limited views about Hispanics to her advantage and created inroads for all other Latinos in the organization? While she may have felt like "the only one" on many occasions, she did not get mad; she got smart. She shared with me,

> I felt isolated many times, but it also challenged me to take on the role as a Latina spokesperson and utilize it to help my community and to utilize it to move up in the organization. Because there were so few of us in the organization, it made me more aware of the importance—even if we don't want to—of taking on that role to advance our community. And as a result of that, I did some pioneering work at that organization and three years later they've expanded my role into a national high-level position that serves the purpose of increasing the number of Latinos in the organization and servicing Latino people through the organization. What was once an isolating incident became a good thing.

CHAPTER TAKEAWAYS
- By the time professionals who were the "only one" could have advanced to senior management, many have left because they grew tired of watching others with fewer qualifications get the better assignments; were edged out for promotions; or were perceived as underperforming and were asked to leave.
- The micro-inequity of feeling isolated directly impacts our social needs and sense of belonging within Mazlow's hierarchy of needs. Being the "only one" increases the chances of feeling invisible. When we are not a part of the social fabric in an organization, it is not difficult to feel excluded.
- Organizations should meaningfully look to their employees for referrals for filling job openings and to participate in interviews and selection committees.

- Of the ten states with the highest percentage of racial minorities, only Texas and Washington, DC, also appeared on the list of states with the highest job growth. Professionals of color who decided to brave isolation and moved to states and cities with job growth are hyper-visible and are often tapped for political and business opportunities by leaders who are eager to support diversity.

Conclusion: Ending on a High Note

In 1993's *The Rage of a Privileged Class*, Ellis Cose wrote that "no other racial group in America had endured as much rejection on the path to acceptance" as African Americans, and they were left staring at the "final door . . . uncertain of admittance." He examined the issues middle class African Americans face and drew attention to the disenfranchisement they continue to experience and the resulting rage they feel when they are left standing outside the "final door."

"After all, it is impossible to solve a problem if the source of that problem is ignored."
—Tim Wise, *Colorblind: The Rise of Post-Racial Politics and the Retreat from Racial Equity*

Looking at the situation twenty years later by interviewing a broader swath of women and racial, cultural, religious, and other minorities, I see convincing arguments that while much has changed, much has remained the same.

In 2003, the Supreme Court of the United States recognized the importance of diversity in today's businesses in the University of Michigan case *Grutter v. Bollinger*. In its decision the Court stated, "American businesses have made clear that the skills needed in today's increasingly global marketplace can only be developed through exposure to widely diverse people, cultures, ideas, and viewpoints" (despite Justice O'Connor's opinion that in twenty-five years, racial preferences to achieve diversity will be superfluous).

If television were society's diversity barometer, there would be very little room to argue that America is not a melting pot. Television shows like *Scandal* and *Grey's Anatomy* feature African American, Asian, and Latino characters as positive role models.

Kenneth Chenault of American Express, Ursula Burns of Xerox, and Sheryl Sandberg of Facebook are just a few of the executives who are shaking up the old boys' club.

Ninety-six companies in the S&P 100 now implement policies prohibiting discrimination based on sexual orientation, and thirty-three have voiced public support of the Employment Non-Discrimination Act (ENDA) that would offer universal protection against discrimination, which would include LGBT employees.[57] Legislative and public support for the LGBT community has only increased. In 2011, Gallup found that 53 percent of Americans did not oppose gay marriage,[58] and thirteen state legislatures and Washington, DC, recognized same-gender marriage at the time this book was written. In 2013, the US Supreme Court eviscerated the Defense of Marriage Act (DOMA), which barred federal recognition of same-gender marriages—denying same-sex couples federal benefits.

The election of Barack Obama as the forty-fourth president of the United States of America confirmed to many that race no longer matters and popularized the term "a post-racial America." After all, during a 2007 speech in Selma, Alabama, President Obama said that our country is 90 percent on the road to racial equality.[59]

Yet, somehow within the last ten years, it became taboo and political to talk about race as an identity with adversity. Diversity has become a euphemism for talking about race and the other minority identities that many of us find difficult to discuss and try to avoid. A Diversity Luncheon or a Diversity Reception has a much nicer sounding ring to some than the Networking Reception to Increase Minority Representation. But that is the real truth that we are going after. Until we are honest about what we are really trying to accomplish, we will not be able to accomplish it.

Although President Obama received 43 percent of the White vote in 2008 and 39 percent in 2012,[60] there was still White hysteria as to whether President Obama would create policies that would inure to the benefit of Blacks at the expense of Whites. When surveyed, 37 percent of Whites and 65 percent of Republicans thought that Obama's policies were more preferential to Blacks than Whites.[61] Glenn Beck, Rush Limbaugh, and a few other conservative personalities fueled fears and suspicions that Whites would be at a disadvantage under a Black president's leadership who would, assumingly, create policies that disproportionately favored Blacks. Race now mattered but to a different audience. All of this vitriol proved that the likelihood of us getting upset with preferential treatment increases as our membership in the favored group decreases.[62]

Race is still a strong category of identity that comes with a history. It is still an area that we are afraid to discuss or feel no longer has impact; however, we are always surprised when we see low representation of Blacks and Hispanics in various professions.[63] According to The Chronicle of Higher Education, "Today's typical college leader is a married White male with a doctorate in education."[64] In law, over 85 percent of law firm partners are White.[65] In medicine, White men continue to make up the majority of doctors.[66] According to *Black Enterprise* magazine, a National Science Foundation study found that "only 15 percent of scientists and engineers were minority men—238,000 were Black men compared with 5 million who were White and 840,000 who were Asian."[67] ABC's hit show *Scandal* is such a big deal not only because of the superb writing, but also because this is the first time in 40 years that an African American has been in the lead role in a network drama.[68]

It is a fallacy to think that race—and the other characteristics that have traditionally marginalized historically underrepresented groups in the workplace—is insignificant to hiring, promotion, and termination decisions. When we look at society at large, subtle and tacit discriminatory policies continue to create a chasm of negative disparities in housing, criminal justice, and health care.

In 2013, the Housing and Urban Development department released a report revealing that racial minorities continue to experience discrimination.[69] Landlords and realtors show Whites more properties, giving Whites more housing options. People of color in affluent White neighborhoods still get head turns and questionable stares asking, "What are they doing here?"

According to the Bureau of Justice Statistics, African Americans are four times more likely than Whites to die during an encounter with the police.[70] In 2012, in New York City where over 121 languages are spoken, the New York City Police Department (NYPD) was entangled in a class action lawsuit filed by the Center for Constitutional Rights alleging that the city's aggressive policy of stopping and frisking residents, visitors, and anyone on the street—without suspicion—violated their Fourth Amendment right to be free from unlawful searches and seizures and their Fourteenth Amendment right to freedom from racial discrimination.[71] From 2004 to 2009, of the 2.8 million stops and frisks, over 50 percent of those stopped were Black; 30 percent were Latinos, and 10 percent were White.[72] In fact, of those stops only about 10 percent resulted in an arrest or summons.[73] Although Blacks and Latinos, combined, comprise 35.5 percent of New York City's population, they represented more than 85 percent of those stopped by the police.[74]

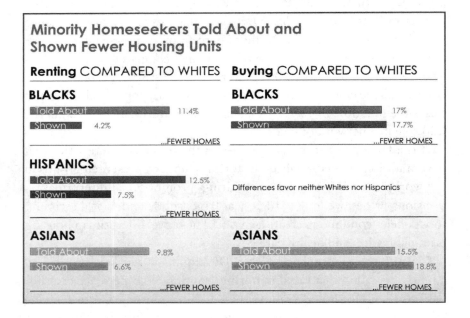

Minority Homeseekers Told About and Shown Fewer Housing Units

Renting COMPARED TO WHITES | **Buying** COMPARED TO WHITES

BLACKS
Told About 11.4%
Shown 4.2%
...FEWER HOMES

BLACKS
Told About 17%
Shown 17.7%
...FEWER HOMES

HISPANICS
Told About 12.5%
Shown 7.5%
...FEWER HOMES

Differences favor neither Whites nor Hispanics

ASIANS
Told About 9.8%
Shown 6.6%
...FEWER HOMES

ASIANS
Told About 15.5%
Shown 18.8%
...FEWER HOMES

In health care, race is the "crucial variable" when determining why some groups have better outcomes than others.[75] In an experiment, medical researchers used two different sets of actors—one Black and one White—who expressed similar health conditions. The researchers found that, "Black male actor-patients, whose symptoms and comments were identical to White male actor-patients, were perceived to be less intelligent, less likely to participate in treatment decisions, and more likely to miss appointments."[76] "Racially biased discretion" is a hurdle where subjective opinions can mean the difference between aggressive treatment and withheld care. Bias in health care can truly be a matter of life or death.

America has been a country where race, gender, national origin, and religious discrimination were legal for over 300 years—more years than the fifty years they have been illegal. It would be naïve to think that the systems and hierarchies that were created around race and other historically disadvantaged demographics have disappeared.

After practicing employment law for six years, I had an "aha" moment about what I wanted to be when I grew up. While facilitating a leadership training session for INROADS, a pipeline organization that trains and develops students of color to enter Corporate America, I realized how much I enjoyed creating educational programs about employee rights and responsibilities in the workplace. I preferred working proactively with groups to create employment education programs that focus on the intersection of diversity issues and career management instead of engaging in hardcore adversarial courtroom battles. So as to not delay the dream, I created my own diversity consulting firm—QUEST Educational Initiatives—and made the permanent switch from practicing law. Today, the majority of my work as a speaker and consultant involves working with corporations, law firms, educational institutions, and community-based organizations to approach diversity by Questioning their Understood Established Societal Training (QUEST). The day I left my firm, I went from being an employment lawyer to a diversity and employment law consultant.

Alas, everything happens for a good reason. As Sam Hamadeh, founder and chief executive of Vault.com, told the December issue of Knowledge@Wharton, "[B]eing an outsider increases the likelihood that someone will want to start his own venture. The more you are part of the establishment, the more you are giving up to start a business." Many of the individuals who participated in this book are highly accomplished women and men who left their organizations to be successful elsewhere. They did not get mad; they got smart.

How you approach inclusion, retention, and working with out-groups will greatly predict how successful your outcomes will be. In social

"One is more likely to learn from challenging or difficult experiences than from non-challenging experiences."[77]

—Rebecca Neel and Jenessa Shapiro, *Is Racial Bias Malleable? Whites' Lay Theories of Racial Bias Predict Divergent Strategies for Interracial Interactions*

psychology, there are two schools of thought about approaching situations. There are entity theorists and incremental theorists, and the only thing that separates their effectiveness is their perspective when tackling difficult encounters with out-groups.[78]

Entity theorists believe that racial bias is fixed and can never change; therefore, they are less curious about out-groups and limit their exposure to them. They could say something insensitive; they could demonstrate their limited knowledge of other groups, although they should be further along the continuum; or they could be ridiculed for lack of awareness. Entity theorists seek to avoid difficult situations because it would be a public revelation of their lack of ability. They avoid working with, mentoring, and socializing with out-groups, ultimately limiting their exposure to out-groups. These are the people who would rather exit an interaction with someone from an out-group as opposed to learning more about the person and understanding his or her perspective. The fear is that they would be found out as being inept in social interactions with out-groups; this is a level of unyielding control and vulnerability that they are not willing to expose. Further, there is less desire to potentially engage in situations where they may say or do something awkward; they are not interested in learning from "negative" experiences.

However, incremental theorists look at interactions with out-groups as an opportunity to learn, gather feedback, and develop tactics and strategies for future encounters. Because incremental theorists believe that racial bias is malleable, they understand that there is room to improve and grow in this area. They see those awkward interactions as "offering diagnostic information about their current and presumably changeable levels of ability, potentially providing useful information about how to be more successful in this domain in the future."[79] Incremental theorists consider the situations that present struggles as opportunities that could lead to advancement. Their goal is never to stay at their current level of understanding but instead to grow. They are open to negative feedback and take a cooperative model of "partner-relevant approach" to learning from difficult encounters. Rather than a "self-relevant approach" where a person is learning to only help themselves (e.g., asking questions that make an out-group member the ambassador of their group), a partner-relevant approach focuses on how a person's biases impacted the out-group member. Partner-relevant examples include asking the out-group member how he or she feeling, checking in with the out-group member to learn more about his or her individual perspective. It is as simple as asking what could or should you do differently in the interaction. Remember in chapter 4 how a male-dominated group learned from their huge mistake when the first woman joined their group and was not allowed to enter the meeting venue because of her gender? Bias is malleable and can be shaped and improved over interactions. Incremental theorists are not afraid of the next challenge. But, you have to be willing to put in the work.

As you digest the testimonials from this book and determine a plan for using them to create a more inclusive and engaging environment, consider who you want to be: a rigid entity theorist who is not willing to accept that you can change or an incremental theorist who is not afraid of change?

CHAPTER TAKEAWAYS

- Diversity has become a placeholder for race that while allowing some to feel more comfortable in conversations around inclusion and access, it creates false notions about present-day discrimination.

> "Love your Enemies, for they tell you your Faults."
> —Benjamin Franklin, *Poor Richard's Almanack*

- Entity theorists believe that racial bias is fixed and can never change; therefore, they are less curious about out-groups and limit their exposure to them. Entity theorists seek to avoid difficult situations because it would be a public revelation of their lack of ability.

- Incremental theorists look at interactions with out-groups as an opportunity to learn, gather feedback, and develop tactics and strategies for future encounters. Because incremental theorists believe that racial bias is malleable, they understand that there is room to improve and grow in this area.

NOTES

1. Susan Antilla, *Sex Harassment at Work Gets Weirder, Scarier*, BLOOMBERG (Aug. 23, 2010), http://www.bloomberg.com/news/2010-08-24/sex-harassment-at-work-gets-weirder-scarier-commentary-by-susan-antilla.html.

2. M. Hewstone, M. Rubin & H. Willis, *Intergroup Bias*, 53 ANN. REV. PSYCHOL. 575 (2002).

3. *Id.* (citing MICHAEL HOGG & DOMINIC ABRAMS, IN GROUP MOTIVATION:SOCIAL PSYCHOLOGICAL PERSPECTIVES 173–90 (1993).

4. *Id.*

5. A. Ivey, W. Liu & T. Pickett, *White Middle-Class Privilege: Social Class Bias and Implications for Training and Practice*, 35 J. MULTICULTURAL COUNSELING & DEV 194 (2007).

6. Justin D. Levinson, *Forgotten Racial Equality: Implicit Bias, Decisionmaking, and Misremembering*, Duke L.J. 57 (2007).

7. HARVARD'S PROJECT IMPLICIT, https://implicit.harvard.edu/implicit/demo/ (last visited October 29, 2013).

8. John R. Tkach & Edgar Barnett, *The Unconscious Mind*, BOZEMAN SKIN CLINIC (May 31, 2012), http://www.bozemanskinclinic.com/rrp/unconscious-mind.php.

9. D. Amodio & P. Devine, *Stereotyping and Evaluation in Implicit Race Bias: Evidence for Independent Constructs and Unique Effects on Behavior*, 91 J. PERSONALITY & SOC. PSYCHOL. 652, 653–59 (2006).

10. *Id.* at 653.

11. Levinson, *supra* note 6, at 352.

12. Levinson, *supra* note 6, at 352.

13. Levinson, *supra* note 6, at 349 (citing HOWARD EHRLICH, THE SOCIAL PSYCHOLOGY OF PREJUDICE: A SYSTEMATIC THEORETICAL REVIEW AND PROPOSITIONAL INVENTORY OF THE AMERICAN SOCIAL PSYCHOLOGICAL STUDY OF PREJUDICE 35 (1973).

14. LU-IN WANG, DISCRIMINATION BY DEFAULT: HOW RACISM BECOMES ROUTINE 46 (2006).

15. J. Darley, M. Norton & J. Vandello, *Casuistry and Social Category Bias*, 87 J. PER-SONALITY & SOC. PSYCHOL. 817, 819 (2004) (citing T. Ito & G. Urland, *Race and Gender on the Brain: Electrocortical Measures of Attention to the Race and Gender of Multiply Categorizable Individuals*, 85 J. PERSONALITY & SOC. PSYCHOL. 616 (2003)).

16. *Id.* at 821.

17. *Id.* at 818.

18. Levinson, *supra* note 6, at 351.

19. Hewstone, *supra* note 2, at 80 (citing JIM SIDANIUS & FELICIA PRATTO, SOCIAL DOMINANCE: AN INTERGROUP THEORY OF SOCIAL HIERARCHY AND OPPRESSION (1999)).

20. R. Banks & R. Ford, *(How) Does Unconscious Bias Matter?*, 58 EMORY L.J. 1053, 1054 (2009).

21. P. Hanges & J. Ziegert, *Employment Discrimination: The Role of Implicit Attitudes, Motivation, and a Climate for Racial Bias*, J. 90 APPLIED PSYCHOL. 553, 554 (2005).

22. Kim Severson, *At Georgia Restaurant, Patrons Jump to Defend a Chef from Her Critics*, N.Y TIMES (June 22, 2013), http://www.nytimes.com/2013/06/23/us/in-the-s outh-many-are-willing-to-forgive-deens-racial-misstep.html?pagewanted=all.

23. Mary Rowe, *Barriers to Equality: The Power of Subtle Discrimination to Maintain Unequal Opportunity*, 3 EMP. RESPONSIBILITIES & RTS. J. 153 (1990).

24. *Id. See also* STEPHEN YOUNG, MICROMESSAGING: WHY GREAT LEADERSHIP IS BEYOND WORDS 27 (2007).

25. Yoji Cole, *What Should You Be Paid to Champion Diversity? A New Salary Survey Revealed*, COMPENSATION RESOURCES (Sept. 21, 2002), http://www.compensationresources .com/press-room/what-should-you-be-paid-to-champion-diversity--a-new-salary-survey-revealed-.php.

26. SOC'Y FOR HUMAN RES. MGMT. & GLOBOFORCE, SHRM/GLOBOFORCE SURVEY: EMPLOYEE RECOGNITION PROGRAMS, FALL 2012 (2012).

27. *State of the American Workplace Employee Engagement Insights for U.S. Business Leaders*, GALLUP, STATE OF THE AMERICAN WORKPLACE: EMPLOYEE ENGAGEMENT INSIGHTS FOR U.S. BUSINESS LEADERS (2013), *available at* http://www.gallup.com/ strategicconsulting/163007/state-american-workplace.aspx (last visited October 29, 2013).

28. *Engagement at Work: Its Effect on Performance Continues in Tough Economic Times*, GALLUP, ENGAGEMENT AT WORK: ITS EFFECT ON PERFORMANCE CONTINUES IN TOUGH ECONOMIC TIMES (2012), *available at* http://www.gallup.com/strategicconsulting/161459

/engagement-work-effect-performance-continues-tough-economic-times.aspx (last visited October 29, 2013).

29. Drew Westen, *How Race Turns Up the Volume on Incivility: A Scientifically Informed Post-Mortem to a Controversy*, Huffington Post (Sept. 23, 2009), http://www .huffingtonpost.com/drew-westen/how-race-turns-up-the-vol_b_295874.html.

30. T. Gilovich, E. Pronin & L. Ross, *Objectivity in the Eye of the Beholder: Divergent Perceptions of Bias in Self Versus Others*, 111 Psychol. Rev. 781 (2004).

31. Luchina Fisher, *Law Partnerships Elude Women of Color*, WeNews (Jan. 29, 2004), http://womensenews.org/story/the-nation/040129/law-partnerships-elude-women-color#.UdceJ3DD9lY.

32. Malcolm Gladwell, Blink: The Power of Thinking Without Thinking (2005).

33. *Id.* at 238.

34. *Id.* at 241.

35. Justin Levinson, *Forgotten Racial Equality: Implicit Bias, Decisionmaking, and Misremembering*, 57 Duke Law Journal 345 (2007).

36. N. Fast, C. Heath & G. Wu, *Common Ground and Cultural Prominence: How Conversation Reinforces Culture*, 20 Psychol. Sci. 904 (2009).

37. Lakshmi Ramarajan & Sigal G. Barsade, What Makes the Job Tough? The Influence of Organizational Respect on Burnout in Human Services (Nov. 2006), *available at* http://knowledge.wharton.upenn.edu/paper.cfm?paperID=1338 (unpublished manuscript).

38. *CareerBuilder Study Finds More Workers Feeling Bullied in the Workplace*, CareerBuilder (Aug. 19, 2012), http://www.careerbuilder.com/share/aboutus/pressreleasesdetail.aspx?sd=8%2f29%2f2012&id=pr713&ed=12%2f31%2f2012.

39. Benedict Carey, *Fear in the Workplace: The Bullying Boss*, N.Y. Times (June 22, 2004), http://www.nytimes.com/2004/06/22/health/fear-in-the-workplace-the-bullying-boss.html.

40. *National Education Association and Alaska Affiliate to Pay $750,000 for Harassment of Women*, U.S. Equal Emp't Opportunity Comm'n (May 22, 2006), http://www.eeoc .gov/eeoc/newsroom/release/5-22-06.cfm.

41. *Highlights: Workplace Stress & Anxiety Disorders Survey*, Anxiety and Depression Ass'n of Am., http://www.adaa.org/workplace-stress-anxiety-disorders-survey (last visited October 29, 2013).

42. *Good Technology Survey Reveals Americans Are Working More, but on Their Own*

Schedule, PRNᴇᴡsWɪʀᴇ (July 2, 2012), http://www.prnewswire.com/news-releases
/good-technology-survey-reveals-americans-working-more-but-on-the
ir-own-schedule-161018305.html.

43. Tara Kelly, *80 Percent of Americans Spend an Extra Day a Week Working after Hours, New Survey Says*, Hᴜꜰꜰɪɴɢᴛᴏɴ Pᴏsᴛ (July 3, 201), http://www.huffingtonpost
.com/2012/07/03/americans-work-after-hours-extra-day-a-week_n_1644527.html.

44. A. Aᴛᴄʜɪsᴏɴ, P. Sᴀɴʙᴏʀɴ & R. Mᴀʟʜᴏᴛʀᴀ, AᴏɴHᴇᴡɪᴛᴛ, Tʀᴇɴᴅs ɪɴ Gʟᴏʙᴀʟ Eɴɢᴀɢᴇᴍᴇɴᴛ Rᴇᴘᴏʀᴛ (2011), *available at* http://www.aon.com/
human-capital-consulting/thought-leadership/compensation/report_global_trends
_employee_engagement.jsp.

45. Jerker Denrell, *Why Most People Disapprove of Me: Experience Sampling in Impression Formation*, Aᴍᴇʀɪᴄᴀɴ Psʏᴄʜᴏʟᴏɢɪᴄᴀʟ Assᴏᴄɪᴀᴛɪᴏɴ Vol. 112 (2005), pp. 951–78.

46. *Forum shopping* is a litigation strategy whereby a party will choose a court that may be more favorable to their claim. In this context, the mid-career attorney is using the term to describe how clients will overlook her and seek other attorneys they think will be more favorable to their issues.

47. Vivia Chen, *Cleary Gottlieb Has a Bad Hair Day*, Lᴀᴡ.ᴄᴏᴍ (Aug. 1, 2007), http://www.law.com/jsp/article.jsp?id=900005556970&Cleary_Gottlieb_Has_a_Bad
_Hair_Day&slreturn=20130706091431.

48. Burlington Northern & Santa Fe Ry. v. White, 548 U.S. 53 (2006).

49. R. Baumeister, E. Bratslavsky, C. Finkenauer & K. Vohs, 5 Bᴀᴅ Is Sᴛʀᴏɴɢᴇʀ Tʜᴀɴ Gᴏᴏᴅ, Rᴇᴠ. Gᴇɴ. Psʏᴄʜᴏʟ. 323 (2001).

50. B. Fredrickson & K. Johnson, *We All Look the Same to Me: Positive Emotions Eliminate the Own-Race Bias in Face Recognition*, 16 Psᴄʏʜᴏʟ. Sᴄɪ. 875, 875–76 (2005) ("Neurophysiological studies have identified specific areas of the brain active in the processing of faces and that the processing of cross-race faces is different from the processing of own-race faces.").

51. Sᴜsᴀɴ Cʜᴏʏ, Nᴀᴛ'ʟ Cᴛʀ. ꜰᴏʀ Eᴅᴜᴄ. Sᴛᴀᴛɪsᴛɪᴄs, NCES 2001-126, Sᴛᴜᴅᴇɴᴛs Wʜᴏsᴇ Pᴀʀᴇɴᴛs Dɪᴅ Nᴏᴛ Gᴏ ᴛᴏ Cᴏʟʟᴇɢᴇ (2001), *available at* http://nces.ed.gov/
pubs2001/2001126.pdf.

52. Abby Ellin, *Under 40, Successful, and Itching for a New Career*, N.Y. Tɪᴍᴇs (Dec. 16, 2006), http://www.nytimes.com/2006/12/16/business/16career.html?_r=0.

53. U.S. Sᴇɴᴀᴛᴏʀ Rᴏʙᴇʀᴛ Mᴇɴᴇɴᴅᴇᴢ, Cᴏʀᴘᴏʀᴀᴛᴇ Dɪᴠᴇʀsɪᴛʏ Rᴇᴘᴏʀᴛ (Aug. 2010), *available at* http://www.menendez.senate.gov/imo/media/doc/
CorporateDiversityReport2.pdf.

54. K. Barton, C. Burns & S. Kerby, *The State of Diversity in Today's Workforce*, WIL-LIAMS INST. (July 12, 2012), http://williamsinstitute.law.ucla.edu/press/the-state-of-d iversity-in-todays-workforce/.

55. Jeffrey Jones, *North Dakota, Midwestern States Lead U.S. in Hiring*, GALLUP ECONOMY (Feb. 6, 2013), http://www.gallup.com/poll/160325/north-dakota-midwe stern-states-lead-hiring.aspx.

56. *State & County QuickFacts*, U.S. CENSUS BUREAU, http://quickfacts.census.gov/ qfd/index.html (last visited October 29, 2013).

57. *Examining the Cracks in the Ceiling: A Survey of Corporate Diversity Practices of the S&P 100*, CALVERT INVESTMENTS (Mar. 2013), http://www.calvert.com/ sr-examining-cracks.html.

58. Frank Newport, *For First Time, Majority of Americans Favor Legal Gay Marriage*, GALLUP NEWS (May 20, 2011), http://www.gallup.com/poll/147662/First-Time-Ma jority-Americans-Favor-Legal-Gay-Marriage.aspx.

59. Lynn Sweet, *Barack Obama Selma speech. Text as delivered*, CHI. SUN-TIMES (Mar. 5, 2007), http://voices.suntimes.com/early-and-often/sweet/ obamas-selma-speech-text-as-de/.

60. Chris Cillizza & Jon Cohen, *President Obama and the White Vote? No Problem*, WASH. POST (Nov. 8, 2012), http://www.washingtonpost.com/blogs/the-fix/wp/2012 /11/08/president-obama-and-the-white-vote-no-problem/.

61. YouGovPolimetrix, THE ECONOMIST/YouGov POLL: AUGUST 16–18, 2009, at 37 (2009), *available at* http://media.economist.com/media/pdf/Tabs20090819.pdf.

62. Elisha Babad, *The Psychological Price of Media Bias*, 11 J. EXP. PSYCHOL.: APPLIED 245 (2005).

63. Nelson D. Schwartz & Michael Cooper, *Racial Diversity Efforts Ebb for Elite Careers, Analysis Finds*, N.Y. TIMES (May 27, 2013), http://www.nytimes.com/2013/05 /28/us/texas-firm-highlights-struggle-for-black-professionals.html?nl=todaysheadlines &emc=edit_th_20130528&_r=0.

64. Jack Stripling, *Survey Finds a Drop in Minority Presidents Leading Colleges*, CHRONICLE OF HIGHER LEARNING (Mar. 12, 2012), http://chronicle.com/article/ Who-Are-College-Presidents-/131138/.

65. Brian Zabcik, *2013 Diversity Scorecard: Firms Regain Lost Ground*, THE AMERI-CAN LAWYER (June 6, 2013), http://www.americanlawyer.com/PubArticleTAL.jsp ?id=1202600856240&2013_Diversity_Scorecard_Firms_Regain_Lost_Ground.

184

66. *Fast Facts: Degrees Conferred by Sex and Race*, NAT'L CTR. FOR EDUC. STATISTICS http://nces.ed.gov/fastfacts/display.asp?id=72 (last visited October 29, 2013).

67. *See* Jaquelina C. Falkenheim & Joan S. Burrelli, *Diversity in Science and Engineering Employment in Industry*, NAT'L SCI. FOUND. (Mar. 2012), http://www.nsf.gov/statistics/infbrief/nsf12311/; Jannelle Rucker, *Close the Gap: Top 5 STEM Job Options for Black Men*, BLACK ENTER. (June 10, 2013), http://www.blackenterprise.com/career/jobs-stem-science-tech-black-male-employment/.

68. Tanzina Vega, *A Show Makes Friends and History: "Scandal" on ABC Is Breaking Barriers*, N.Y. TIMES (Jan. 16, 2013), http://www.nytimes.com/2013/01/17/arts/television/scandal-on-abc-is-breaking-barriers.html?pagewanted=all&_r=0.

69. CLAUDIA ARANDA ET AL., HOUSING DISCRIMINATION AGAINST RACIAL AND ETHNIC MINORITIES 2012 (2013), *available at* http://www.huduser.org/portal/publications/fairhsg/hsg_discrimination_2012.html.

70. *See also* R. Banks, J. Eberhardt & L. Ross, *Discrimination and Implicit Bias in a Racially Unequal Society*, 94 CALIF. L. REV. 1169, 1172 (2006) ("In a recent series of experimental studies, Eberhardt and colleagues examined the psychological association between race and criminality. In one study, they exposed police officers to a group of Black faces or a group of White faces and asked, 'Who looks criminal?' They found that police officers not only viewed more Black faces than White faces as criminal, but also viewed those Black faces rated as the most stereotypically Black (e.g., those with wide noses, thick lips, or dark skin) as the most criminal of all.")

71. Floyd v. City of New York, 2012 U.S. Dist. LEXIS 68676 (S.D.N.Y. 2012) (Shira A. Scheindlin U.S.D.J.) (class certification decision case alleging unconstitutional stops by the NYPD disproportionally impacting Blacks and Latinos).

72. *Id.*

73. Al Baker, *Judge Grants Class-Action Status to Stop-and-Frisk Suit*, N.Y. TIMES (May 12, 2012), http://cityroom.blogs.nytimes.com/2012/05/16/judge-allows-class-action-status-in-stop-and-frisk-lawsuit/?_r=0.

74. *State & County QuickFacts: New York*, U.S. CENSUS BUREAU, http://quickfacts.census.gov/qfd/states/36000.html (last visited October 29, 2013).

75. MICHAEL K. BROWN ET AL., WHITEWASHING RACE: THE MYTH OF A COLOR-BLIND SOCIETY 47 (2005).

76. *Id.* at 48.

77. R. Neel & J. Shapiro, *Is Racial Bias Malleable? Whites' Lay Theories of Racial Bias*

Predict Divergent Strategies for Interracial Interactions, 103 J. PERSONALITY & SOC. PSY-
CHOL. 101, 102 (2012).

    78. *Id.* at 101.

    79. *Id.*

INDEX